A STUDY OF SELECTED BRITISH DYSTOPIAN NOVELS

by

SATHIYARAJAN.N

PREFACE

The first chapter is the **Introduction**. It throws light on describing the salient features of dystopian novels in general. It also highlights the four novels taken up for study and the biographical details of the respective writers. The novels taken up for study are Aldous Huxley's *Brave New World*, George Orwell's *Nineteen Eighty – Four,* Anthony Burgess' *A Clockwork Orange* and P. D. James's *The Children of Men.*

The second chapter discusses Aldous Huxley's novel *Brave New World* in detail as a dystopian one. The novel opens in the building of the central London Hatchery. The conditioning centre happens to be the world state's motto 'community', 'identity' and 'stability'. The director explains to the students how mass production of hatcheries has been made possible by means of artificial insemination and fertilisation of eggs. Five types of beings are produced in the hatchery. The superior ones are called Alphas and Betas and the inferior ones are called Gammas, Deltas and Epsilons.

The publication of the novel *Nineteen Eighty-Four* has won George Orwell, name and fame and the third chapter discusses it as a dystopian novel. The book is a frightening portrait of a totalitarian society where love is punished, privacy is lost and truth is distorted. He uses a grim tone to differentiate from his other novel *Animal Farm* which is a satire on the communist government of the Soviet Union under Stalin. *Nineteen Eighty-Four* is written in the custom of the Utopian novel, and is perhaps best defined as a dystopian novel; literally the opposite of a perfect society.

Anthony Burgess's *A Clockwork Orange* is well discussed in the fourth chapter. The British novelist is considered to be one of the newest and most talented of the younger British writers. The ability of an individual to make moral choices is the major theme of *A Clockwork Orange.* The society presented by Burgess deals with experiments and behaviour modification techniques on criminals. The citizens should be given the choice between the good and the evil. The state should not interfere and destroy the capacity for choice. Burgess points out that destroying the ability to choose evil also destroys the capacity to choose good. In the name of justice and security, the state also commits violence just like Alex and his gang members.

The fourth novel taken up for study is P. D. James's *The Children of Men* and this forms the fifth chapter. The setting for *The Children of Men*, a dystopian novel is a world of mass infertility. The novelist vents her anger against the decline and fall of the modern world, using Dr. Theo as her mouth piece. Narrated in both first person and third person, the novel begins in the year 1995, known as the Year Omega. The fall in the population is due to various reasons, such as birth control, abortion and the spread of AIDS.

The final chapter is the **Conclusion** which discusses the findings of the previous chapters. The earlier chapters have well analysed, the discussed novels as dystopian ones. The novels taken up for study are viewed in the dystopian perspective and proved to be one. The three main aspects that are dealt in dystopian novels are the powerful authority, the oppression of an individual, and the threat of punishment and death. These main characteristics of dystopian fiction issue a certain warning against the possible future of the people.

CONTENTS

ALDOUS HUXLEY
(1894 -1963)

GEORGE ORWELL
(1903- 1950)

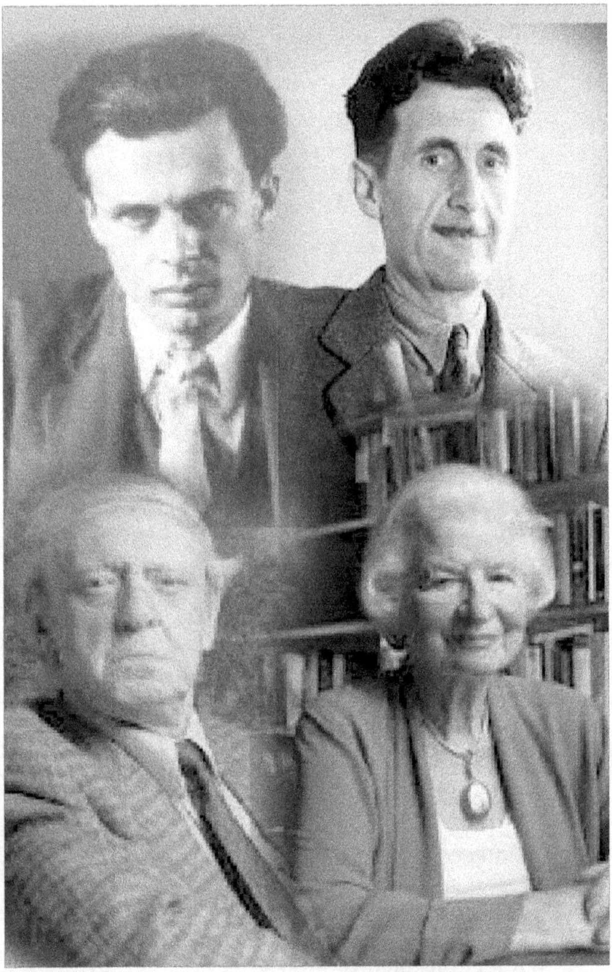

ANTHONY BURGESS
(1917-1913)

P. D.JAMES
(1920-2013)

INTRODUCTION

The word 'dystopia' consists of the Greek prefix 'dys'. It means ill, bad or abnormal. To quote from the Oxford Dictionary, the definition of dystopia is, "an imagined place or state in which everything is unpleasant or bad, typically a totalitarian or environmentally degraded one". Many authors have tried to describe this genre. Gottileb, in the book *Dystopian Fiction East and West, Universe of Terror and Trial,* presents the following definition of a typical dystopian world as:

> A hell on earth, an absurd, death-bound social-political system where the elite deliberately conspires against its own people, against the most universal principles of justice, with emphasis on nightmarish rigged trials, with make believe accusations, followed by all-too-real sentences to hard labour or death. (18)

Dystopian novels examine the fate of an individual in a technologically advanced society. 'Utopia' is defined as an ideally perfect place, especially in its social, political, and moral aspects. The exact definition, given in the Oxford dictionary for Utopia is, 'an imagined place or state of things in which everything is perfect. Misplaced faith in political Utopias has led to ruin'.

Utopian works sketch a future that sees the everyday life of the human beings and an advanced civilisation. Critics have examined the extreme historical circumstances that have taken place during the twentieth century. These historical events have paved the way for flourishing of the dystopian fiction. Many critics point out that some of the finest dystopian works have been produced during the Nazi era in Germany and during the Stalin era in Russia. Various wars over the decade and a commentary upon different totalitarian regimes have provided the scope for the dystopian novels. The typical characteristics of the dystopian fiction are lack of personal freedom, lack of freewill, the value of individual resistance to dictatorships and the power of technology to transform the lives of the people. After the World War II, the dystopian fiction has become more widespread and popular. Janet Witalec, the editor of *Contemporary Literature,* points out the common themes found in dystopian fiction:

> … include mastery of nature to the point that it becomes barren, or turns against humankind; technological advances that enslave humans or regiment their lives; the mandatory division of people in society into castes or groups with specialised functions; and a collective loss of memory and history making mankind easier to manipulate psychologically and ultimately leading to dehumanization. (1)

Aldous Huxley, George Orwell, H. G. Wells, Margaret Atwood, Anthony Burgess and Yevgeny Zamyatin are considered to the most important classic authors in the dystopian literature. Huxley's *Brave New World* (1932), Orwell's *Nineteen Eighty-Four* (1949), H.G Well's *A Modern Utopia* (1904), and Zamyatin's *We* (1924) are supposed to be the major canon works of twentieth century dystopian literature. The modern dystopian authors like Chinua Achebe, Ursula K. Le Guin, Isaac Asimov, Kurt Vonnegut, and Ray Bradbury are greatly influenced by these pioneers and their works. The new generations of contemporary writers like Suzette Haden Elgin, Zoë Fairbairns, and Vlady

Kocinacich have also been inspired by these dystopian writers. Throughout the twentieth century, the dystopian novel has remained critically and commercially successful. The dystopian tradition has been continued and expanded by them. The critics Calin Andrei Mihailescu and James W. Bittner have examined the techniques of the dystopian writers. The writers, in order to create a sense of reality in their works, have indeed balanced recognisable, everyday detail with elements of science fiction and used many techniques. The strongest modern trend in dystopian criticism has been to explore dystopias from a feminist perspective. Many critics including Karen F. Stein, Jocelyn Harris, Kathryn M. Grossman, Peter Fitting, and Elizabeth Mahoney have discussed this feminist perspective in detail. The twentieth century has seen a vivid portrayal of dystopias and works of fiction. They depict not an ideal future but a future as terrible as could be imagined.

Postcolonial writers are in the construction of cultural identities for their new societies. They include strong utopian essentials in their work. On the other hand, actual experience in the postcolonial world has been anything but utopian. It may not be entirely surprising that recent postcolonial literature has taken a powerfully dystopian turn. This experience is particularly pronounced in African fiction. The works containing strong dystopian features have been produced by authors as diverse as Nuruddin Farah's *Variations on the Theme of an African Dictatorship* from Somalia, Ngugiwa Thiong's *Devil on the Cross* from Kenya, Ousmane Sembène's *The Last of the Empire* from Senegal, AyiKwei Armah's *The Beautiful Ones Are Not Yet Born* from Ghana, Henri Lopes' *The Laughing Cry* from the Congo, Hama Tuma's *The Case of the Socialist Witchdoctor* from Ethiopia, Chinua Achebe's *Anthills of the Savannah* from Nigeria and

Wole Soyinka's *Season of Anomy* also from Nigeria. M. Keith Booker in *African Literature and the World System: Dystopian Fiction, Collective Experience, and the Postcolonial Condition* gives an overview:

> Western imaginative literature has also taken a decidedly dystopian turn in the twentieth century, but these African dystopian fictions differ from their European counterparts in certain important ways. … dystopian fiction has become a paradigmatic expression of the Western imagination in the twentieth century, a fact that poses significant problems (and opportunities) for African writers who seek to explore their own specific cultural situations within this genre. (58)

African writers of dystopian fiction face special complications in their attempts to explore new cultural identities. American writers of the 1930s have faced difficulties. Barbara Foley in *Radical Representations: Politics and Form in US Proletarian Fiction* provides a convenient summary of the characteristics of the bourgeois novel including,

> tendency of realistic narrative to dissolve contradiction in the movement toward closure; its characteristic opposition of the social to the personal, and its displacement of social critique onto personal ethical choice; its insistence upon the uniqueness, and often the superiority, of its protagonist(s); its co-optation of the reader into agreement with the discourse occupying the apex of the text's implied hierarchy of discourses. (261)

The relationship between dystopia and utopia is termed as intertextual. It is mediated always through a utopian `no place'. This relationship is characterised by Krishan Kumar in *Utopia and Anti-Utopia in Modern Times* as "a chain of challenge and response" (128), with utopia laying down the challenge to which dystopia provides the response. 'Anti-Utopia', is a term which Kumar considers synonymous with dystopia; he claims that it is,

> formed by utopia, and feeds parasitically on it. It depends for its survival on the persistence of utopia. Utopia is the original, anti-utopia the copy - only, as it were, always colored black. It is utopia that provides the positive content to which anti-utopia makes the negative response. (100)

According to this view, dystopia or indeed any of the harmful archetypes of utopia listed above is generated only in response to utopian textual stimuli. Dystopia is a reaction or response to an extension of utopian literature, or utopian political tracts, rather than a response to an existing actuality.

The contemporary approach to dystopia, is to admit, encourage, and explore both its relevance to the concrete, real world. This essential shift in the critical focus on dystopia, a move from reading dystopia as social imagination to dystopia as social reality has allowed critics to evaluate really and comment on the real world. M. Keith Booker, for example, takes this aspect in his book, *The Dystopian Impulse in Modern Literature: Fiction as Social Criticism,* where he explains at the outset:

> I wish to underscore the role of dystopian fiction as social criticism. In particular, I emphasize throughout this study that the treatment of

> imaginary societies ….in the best dystopian fiction is always highly relevant more or less directly to specific "real world" societies and issues. (18-19)

Tom Moylan remarks in *Scraps of the Untainted Sky: Science Fiction, Utopia, Dystopia* that Dystopia has, “produced challenging cognitive maps of the historical situation by way of imaginary societies that are even worse than those that lie outside their authors and readers' doors” (xi). He further continues:

> Its very textual machinery invites the creation of alternative worlds in which the historical pace time of the author can be re-presented in a way that foregrounds the articulation of its economic, political, and cultural dimensions. [D]ystopian critique can enable its writers and readers to find their way within - and sometimes against and beyond - the conditions that mask the very causes of the harsh realities in which they live. (xii)

The three main aspects that are dealt in dystopian novels are the powerful authority, the oppression of individual, and threat of punishment and death. These main characteristics of dystopian fiction issue a certain warning against the possible future of the people. Kaplan in his article, “The Advert of Literary Dystopia” published in *Extrapolation* says,

> …characteristics of dystopia is a certain ‘political system’. It is described as one of several types of governments and political systems…. These systems include for instance capitalism, communism, fascism,

> totalitarianism, dictatorship and other forms of social, political or economical control. These governments promote great power over citizens. (200)

The state denies the bonds of private loyalty. It enforces absolute obedience to the state. A quasi -religious worship and a state ideology is expected from the society. Gottlieb in *Dystopian fiction East and West: Universe of Terror and Trail* says that, "The overall effect is that actions and emotions that were previously associated with the individuals' private world suddenly become public domain, fully under the punitive control of the state machine" (12). The experience and fate of the protagonist is tragic. It deals with loss on the personal level and faces worse possibilities than loss of life. He loses his position, freedom, his beloved, and his private, individual identity. He realises that something in the society is false. He is confident that he can change these conditions for better. The threat of death does not discourage him that is forbidden by the regime.

The dystopian fiction of the western model portrays the protagonist, awakening to a kind of love. Gottlieb points out that, "falling in love with a woman who offers affections, passion or simply an intimate bond" (21), helps a lot. His love protects his individuality and unique private world. Dystopia advises the societies to neglect ideals of romantic love. The characters also do not give importance to the activity. The protagonist's another important feature is the pursuit of history concerned with the vital importance of a record of the past. As Gottlieb says,

> One of the most typical messages of dystopian fiction is that access to the records of the past is vital to the mental health of any society. The reason

> is simple and clear. Protagonists are eager to obtain and hold on to a genuine record of the past, a past the totalitarian regime would like to distort or deny completely. (12)

He lives on different time-plane. His definition of the past happens to be the present of the reader at the time this satire is written. It is a warning issued by the author to the reader. Gottlieb issues a warning that, "Beware: the protagonist's present could become your future" (15).

The hero, who wants to fight against the government, hopes to get a support from the likeminded people. He makes an effort to escape from suppression. He is not successful and is forced to compromise with the society or government. Some dystopian novels depict the successful hero, who manages to solve the conflict with the superior power and changes things for his benefits. Maria Varsam rightly asserts in her article, "Concrete Dystopia: Slavery and Its Others" that, "whereas . . . utopia is a manifestation of desire and hope for a better world and an 'unalienated order' that upsets the status quo, . . . dystopia delineates the crushing of hope and the displacement of desire for the purpose of upholding that status quo" (209).

Technology has been on the rise during the nineteenth century. There has been an accumulation of different opinions. People have become aware of the danger of scientific process along with the benefits of it. New ideas in the ideological and philosophical domain have contributed towards skepticism and dystopian thinking. Nietzsche's mistrust of scientific pursuits in general is seen in his *The Birth of Tragedy* written in 1871. He asks a series of questions like this:

> Indeed, what does all scientific enquiry in general mean considered as a symptom of life? What is the point of all that science and, even more serious, where did it come from? What about that? Is scientific scholarship perhaps only a fear and an excuse in the face of pessimism, a delicate self-defence against -- the Truth? And speaking morally, something like cowardice and falsehood? Speaking unmorally, a clever trick? (6)

The twentieth century has derived a kind of comport and support in reading dystopian novels which are pessimistic. People identify themselves with the protagonist, who lives in the nightmare and they also want to take efforts to fight with the oppressor. They can predict the future in a totalitarian regime. They are made aware that advanced technology can play a major role in their lives.

Darko Suvin in an article, "Metamorphoses of Science Fiction: On the Poetics and History of a Literary Genre, in *The real Utopia* defines Utopia as a verbal construction of a particular quasi-human community where sociopolitical institutions, norms, and individual relationships are organized according to a more perfect principle than in the author's community" (4). Suvin is especially concerned with seeing Utopia as a literary form. The credit goes to Plato and his *Republic* written around 380 B.C. It has given birth to the genre that is known the Utopian literature. The word Utopia is translated from a Greek word which means 'no place'. In English it can be interpreted as 'good place'. It has double meaning which brings out many definitions. Martin Plattel in his work,

Utopian and Critical Thinking, suggests that, "the utopian searches of happiness, dream of a new earthly paradise, in which an authentic freedom reigns and happiness is sought in unbridled sensuous delight" (47).

At the beginning of the sixteenth century, Thomas More, an English humanist and statesman has coined the word 'Utopia'. He uses the same word as the title of his book. An image of an ideal state, an organised society, rules, values, and laws are depicted in his work. He exposes the flaw of English society of his time. He criticises and contrasts it with the idea of an ideal state. In More's state of Utopia, everyone enjoys freedom of speech. It is not considered to be a crime. Tolerance is a necessary condition for any ideal state. Citizens are allowed to worship and to believe their gods. The citizens are given their chance to maintain their individuality and independence. George Kateb in *Utopia and Its Enemies*, offers a more detailed description of the Utopian society: all conflicts of conscience and conflicts of interest are abolished:

> . . . all the obstacles to a decent life for all men have been removed, . . . the resource fullness of modern technology is put in the unfettered service of lessening labor and increasing and enriching labor," with "peace, abundance, and virtue permanently and universally obtained. (17)

Work suppresses their freewill. The utopian law punishes all the lazy citizens. The people have to work for six hours. Even in the leisure time they are not allowed to be idle and indulge in useless activities. The leisure time is also made to be useful by doing something beneficial instead of wasting the long hours of the precious time. After all, everyone is aware of the wonderful proverb that 'time and tide wait for no man'. No mortal being can ever rewind the clock of time. Once gone, it is gone forever and no amount of tear shedding or pleading is going to bring it back. According to David Harvey in *Spaces of Hope*, "Utopia is an artificially created island, which functions as an isolated, coherently organized, and largely closed space economy" (160). Another comparison of dystopia and utopia are 'violence and war'. The utopian ruler and his citizens want to live in peace and mutual solitude.

Aldous Leonard Huxley, the English writer is one of the prominent members of the Huxley families. He is well known for his novels and essays. He has been successful as a short story writer and poet. His travelogues, film stories and scripts have brought name and fame. Huxley has made his mark as an examiner and a critic of social morals and ideals. He is a humanist. He has turned his attention to spiritual subjects and philosophical mysticism towards the end of his life. Huxley is readily accepted as one of the eminent intellectuals of his time. His science fiction *Brave New World* (1932) is the novel that has brought him immediate recognition and appreciation. Margaret Atwood in her "Introduction" to the novel quotes from, *The Tempest* which is the source of Huxley's title: "We are such stuff / As dreams are made on. He might well have added: and nightmares" (xiv).

Aldous Leonard Huxley has been born in 1894 in Godalming, England. His father Leonard is a doctor and his mother Julia is the niece of the great poet Mathew Arnold. Huxley has contracted an eye disease at the age of sixteen. Due to this he could not pursue a medical career. His family background, and his own interests, and his scientific training has indeed become an important part of his writing. Huxley regrets missing some of that training during his blindness. He has felt that the training would have helped him to live better in the world of the twentieth century. He has been able to read with the aid of magnifying glass after recovering from his blindness. He has succeeded in getting his degree in English Literature from Oxford University. His brother Julian has written *Aldous Huxley 1894–1963: a Memorial Volume,* where he says, "I believe his blindness was a blessing in disguise. For one thing, it put paid to his idea of taking up medicine as a career ... His uniqueness lay in his universalism. He was able to take all knowledge for his province" (22).

Huxley's early life has been full of tragic events. His mother has died of cancer when he has been about twelve years old. After some years his brother, Trevelyan has committed suicide. Huxley has described the pain that he has experienced over the loss of his mother and brother in his novel *Eyeless in Gaza* (1936). During his stay at Oxford University he has written poems and published three volumes of poetry. After finishing his studies he has become the second assistant editor of the magazine *Athenaeum*, to which he has been contributing regularly. He has been married to Maria Nys. In 1920 he has published his first volumes of short stories called *Limbo* and in 1921 *Crome Yellow*, his first novel has been published. He has travelled to many countries and during his visit to Italy, he has met D.H. Lawrence and has become his intimate friend. In 1938 he has gone to the United States and settled down there permanently in Los Angeles, California. He has died of cancer in 1963.

Huxley has started his novelistic career with the publication of his first novel *Crome Yellow*. This has been followed by *Antic Hay* published in 1923. *Those Barren Leaves,* his third novel, has been published in 1925. His next novel, *Point Counter Point,* is a novel of ideas in the real sense. It is also a psychological novel. His *Brave New World* is a description of his vision of the dystopian future. His novel *Eyeless in Gaza* (1936) and *Island* (1962) reveal his mysticism. His other novels *Time Must Have a Stop* (1944), *After Many Summer* (1939), *Ape and Essence* (1948) and *The Genius and the Goddess* (1955) have followed one after another.

Huxley is a prolific writer. He has published his first collection of verse *The Burning Wheel* in1916, soon after getting a first class in English language and literature at Balliol College, Oxford in 1916. Huxley's first novel contains references of several incidents from his sojourn of Cardington. *Crome Yellow* is not known for its powerful story or plot construction. It presents the character of a poet, named Denis, who comes to Crome, the country house of Mr. Henry and Mrs. Wimbush, where he meets Mr. Scogan a diabolical rationalist, who exhorts him to give up his romantic notions. Huxley's *Crome Yellow* remains the most optimistic novel. The aimless romantic melancholy of the youth, biting irony which do not spare any foible or human passion are intricately woven to create artificial ambience and inimitable intonations. This novel, with all its shortcomings of the first attempt, is a powerful expression of its author's faith in art which has not violated all powerful, undying ideal.

Huxley's second novel *Antic Hay* has satire as its primary object. The characters typify the English intellectuals of 1920s whose attitude has been shaped by war. The theme of disillusionment is the center of the novel. Theodore Gumbril Jr. is recognised as the cynical version of Denis Stone. Gumbril's failure in arts and commerce is a version of Scogan's vision of future without art and poetry. Boldero represents the capitalists. He is willing to buy or sell, or handle anything if there is money in it. Huxley shows the relation of art with life. Gumbril Sr. admits that he does not love his fellow, but he tries to save his image as a good man. He can distinguish good from evil. He dons his mistake to present an image which will match with the style and mannerisms of the Antic Hay. Huxley's *Antic Hay* is a powerful satire, and it has inspired the later novelists of the same genre.

Huxley's third novel *Those Barren Leaves* (1925) has been highly praised in spite of lengthy descriptions of the scenes, and diffused and disrupted discussions. Huxley presents a group of characters who indulge in endless discussions. The novel is set in the Italian Palace of a rich woman, named Mrs. Aldwinkle, who tries to dominate over all things. The story does not have any hero or any story running from cover to cover. It has four love stories told by one to keep the readers' interest alive. Huxley has made a new experiment in plot construction in this novel. As it is said above, it is a collection of four stories. He has interestingly portrayed even a character's autobiography in part II under the heading “Autobiography of Francis Chelifer". The comedy and deception in love make it an interesting reading. The aim of the novelist is simply to present a picture of the ills and evils that has beset the society.

Huxley's *Point Counter Point* (1928) is a better constructed novel than the two earlier ones. The writer has chosen to present various forms and aspects of love through conversations among the characters. Huxley has drawn characters from several different strata of the society to present a comprehensive view of social conditions of those times. The different characters have different attitude to love. *Point Counter Point* is a collection of brilliant satirical sketches which present a fantastic picture of contemporary social manners. While adhering to the formal principles of realism and character as a complex organism, Huxley has moved closer to the modernist's indifference to the material world. Lionel Stevenson observes that *Point Counter Point* lampoons high society, intellectual circles and the Bohemian works. The novel has abundance of imagery of animals, birds and insects. It is held in novel's several debates that man is essentially a beast precariously set in the eggshell of civilisation.

Huxley has started to live in aboard from 1923 onwards. He has described his experiences in his forthcoming novels. In *Along The Road* (1925) subtitled as *Notes and Essays of a Tourist,* Huxley has given a lively account of the places and the works of art he has seen. His third collection of stories is *Little Mexican* (1924). His *Proper Studies* (1927) is the most important of his four volumes of essays, since he has chosen to write in a strong language against vulgarity and perversity of civilisation. In his *Jesting Pilate* (1926) Huxley has recounted his experience in America. He has been shocked to find radical revolution of values of life. Huxley's *Eyeless in Gaza* (1936) is a very spiritual story of a sensual and self indulgent man with a philosophical bent. Huxley tells the story of the man Antony Beavis through a series of flashbacks. Anthony grows to manhood during the World War I and II. He is initially interested in satisfying his lust, but as he grows he becomes conscious of his responsibilities to the society. He helps Dr. Miller in propagation of his peace views, and draws satisfaction and peace from his active participation in social life. The novelist's technique of using of flashbacks, of movements from present to past and past to present brings him closer to the contemporary novelists' technique of stream of consciousness.

Huxley's *After Many a Summer* has been written in 1939. The novel is set against the background of Hollywood films and it is satirical. An American multi-millionaire Joe Stoyte , who has a passion for sensual pleasures, desires to prolong his life as far as possible. He approaches Dr. Obispo, to conduct research to prolong the duration of his life. He is ready to finance the expenses for the project. Huxley warns the readers that too long a life will bring nothing but frustration and disappointment. Huxley's *Time Must Have a Stop* (1944) is also written in America. Huxley has seen the corrupting influence of wealth. Naturally this novel has become a satirical comedy. This novel presents the story of Sebastian Barnack and his uncle Eustace. Although the novel has been written in America, the characters are European. The principal characters, namely, uncle Eustace, Mr. Gamble, Sebastian and Veronic have been treated rather satirically. The novel on the whole, presents various threads of closely and intricately intertwined texture.

Huxley's *Ape and Essence* (1948) describes a gloomy picture of the future of mankind. It presents the fantastic world of baboons and apes. The title of the novel is taken from Shakespeare's *Measure for Measure*. It depicts an imaginary picture of California after the Third World War. The world, Huxley thinks, will be ruled by apes, not human beings, deprived of moral values. In such a world women are hated but not loved. Huxley derides the modern ideas and feels that the future that waits such a generation will dangerously ignore the human value if the apes like men continue to be in power. In Huxley's *The Genius and The Goddess* (1955), the narrator of the story John Rivers himself is one of the participating characters of the novel. All the characters assemble in the house of the Maartens in which the entire action takes place. In spite of the guffaws, the novel remains gloomy and pessimistic. The novel presents the story of Henry Maartens and his wife who are the genius and the goddess respectively. Although Henry is a genius and a Nobel Prize winner, he fails to respond to the emotional and physical needs of his wife. The wife is emotional and sensual while the husband is intellectual. The humiliation of the husband at the hands of his wife goes to show the importance of primeval sensuality in conjugal happiness. Huxley has, in his usual manner, derided science and its demoralising effect upon humanity in general.

Huxley's *Island* (1962) presents a Utopian picture of life in Pala, an island on the South Sea. Unlike *Brave New World* it inspires with a positive Utopian dream. The society depicted in it, consists of a few ideal persons like Dr. Robert Mac Phail who makes sincere efforts to improve the society. Huxley takes the opportunity to present his own Utopia, his long cherished ideas on various social and political issues. It presents Huxley's vision of a happy society, governed by benevolent rulers. In this island, the people have freedom to live according to their tastes and temperament, without being conditioned or divided in classes and castes. In this novel Huxley has tried to give his own solution of to several problems that has confronted the society. In his last published work *Literature and Science* he pleads for a harmonious blending of the two. Aldous Huxley has died of cancer on 22nd November, 1963 at his home in Hollywood.

Eric Arthur Blair, who has written his books under the pen-name of George Orwell, has born in 1903 in Motihari, Bengal, in India. He has spent the first four years of his life in India and has been then sent to England for his schooling. He is the second child of Richard Walmesley Blair and Ida Mabel Limouzine. His father has been at that time an agent in the Opium Department of the Indian Civil Service. His paternal grandfather has served in the Indian Army and he has later become a clergyman. His maternal grandfather is a timber-merchant in Burma and later a rice-grower. Eric Arthur Blair has been four years old when the family returned to England and settled at a place called Henley-on-Thames. His father Richard Blair has continued to work in India until his retirement in 1912. Eric Blair has attended the local primary school at Henley-on-Thames and has lived in the strange atmosphere. Eric Blair or George Orwell later has written that even while at home his early childhood has not altogether been happy. Orwell himself says that he knows very well that one has to love his father but the novelist accepts that he merely dislikes his father. Nor does he feel any deep affection for his mother too.

Orwell has been separated from his family and sent to a mediocre preparatory school called St. Cyprian's Sussex. He has later written that one of the codes of this school has been "an almost neurotic dread of poverty, and above all, the assumption that money and privilege are the things that matter" (78). Orwell's essay, called *Such, Such were the Joys* contains Orwell's memories of his life at St. Cyprian's. This essay has been written in 1948, but has been published only after his death because the memories recorded in it are not only unpleasant but also too painful. Orwell in this essay has depicted his school as a reactionary and barbaric Victorian institution. Some of Orwell's other writings, besides this essay also reflects his painful childhood experiences. It seems that oppression and humiliation have formed the dominant pattern of his personal life during his stay at this school. Indeed, the vivid memories of his school days have always haunted Orwell. The novel *Nineteen Eighty-Four*, particularly, reflects the harmful effects of his life at this school. Most of the terrors depicted in this novel are derived from his school experiences.

The next four and a half years have been spent at Eton. There, Aldous Huxley has taught English and French. Huxley's influence on Orwell is very limited. He has been a mediocre student. There has been no sign that one day he would become one of the most influential writers of the twentieth century. He has been poor even at games, though he did serve in the Officers Training Corps. His aversion for study has compelled him to choose a different career altogether. He has appeared, for a competitive examination and has been appointed for the Burmese police. During his brief career in the Burmese police he has recorded his experiences in *A Hanging, Shooting an Elephant*, and *Burmese Days*. In the summer of 1929 Orwell has written several short stories and two novels which he could not publish. Being short of money, he has worked for ten weeks as a dish-washer in a luxury hotel. His experience among the poor of London and Paris now has become the subject of his first book, *Down and Out in Paris and London,* which has been published in 1933, under the pen-name of George Orwell.

Orwell's *Burmese Days* may be regarded as a quite straight forward novel, using autobiographical material. The strongest single impression conveyed in this novel is of loneliness; a solitude which is the cause of bitter pain and unsatisfied longing. The central character, Flory is an English timber merchant in Burma of British Imperial rule. He realises the hypocrisy of imperialism. He knows that his colleagues' values are shallow and narrow though he himself has nothing to offer in their place. He wants to recreate Burmese national character and return the country to its primitive culture, something which the native politicians, do not want to do. Under the pressures of the system Flory's moral character has deteriorated as well, and believes that his only hope for survival is Elizabeth Lackersteen's love. He is painfully wrong about her. He sees that all she desires is to find a respectable husband and to become a Burmese mem- shaib. When Elizabeth eventually rejects him, his last hope disappears and he is overcome by despair. This novel and its central character are based on Orwell's own experience in Burma where he has served as a police officer.

After going back to England, Orwell has contributed literary reviews to a magazine, called *Adelphi*. His journalistic output is enormous. In less than twenty years he has produced more than seven hundred magazine articles, besides his books. Orwell's *A Clergyman's Daughter,* has appeared in 1935 and in this novel the central character finds the strength for endurance after a contact with the working class. Dorothy Hare, the only daughter of a widowed Anglican Curate, has built her life and faith on weak, rigid habits. She lives, like automation, by religious catch phrases. A sudden loss of memory, however, deprives Dorothy of all imaginary props, namely her faith and her routine parish duties, which have given some sort of order to her life. The real failure of *A Clergyman's Daughter* is Orwell's inability to find the correct form to embrace his experience and embody his ideas. Although the book is a failure as a novel, some of its parts are considered to be successful.

Orwell's *Keep the Aspidistra Flying,* (1936) is a novel where the central character is Gordon Comstock who tries to defy the society, as Orwell himself did, by embracing failure. Comstock, the last member of a middle-class family, feels that there is nothing in contemporary society to equal his talents. He surrenders due to self pity and defeatism. He realises that one cannot control one's life; an admission that one can no longer control one's own life. Orwell portrays loneliness and poverty. In 1936 he has been also commissioned by the Left Book Club to write about the economic and social conditions in the depressed industrial regions of northern England. He spent three months gathering material for the book called *The Road to Wigan Pier* which has been published in 1937.In June 1936, Orwell gets married to Eileen O'Shaughnessy, a rather frail but attractive student of psychology who is sophisticated, fastidious, highly intelligent and an intellectual. He has gone to Spain and fought as a volunteer in the Civil War. His wife also has joined him in Spain. All the events and his experiences have become the subject of one of his best books, called *Homage to Catalonia* which has been published in 1938.

In March 1938, Orwell fell ill with tuberculosis, a disease from which he has been suffering as a child. He and his wife have spent the winter of 1938 in Morocco where he has written the book *Coming Up for Air* which has been published in the following year 1939. It demonstrates Orwell's feeling of hopelessness in the face of the approaching conflict. However, George Bowling's humour and his joy in life relieve the gloom of this novel, and the epigraph is taken from a popular song: "He's dead, but he won't lie down". More significantly, Orwell expresses a central aspect of his socialism in this novel. Up to this point he has based his politics on a combination of working and middle class virtues guided by the intellectual, who has maintained his roots. To a great extent, he seems to have realised that his unity is vulnerable to certain world forces at the end of thirties. The modern world, characterised by collapsing boundaries and national cultures has threatened to obliterate individuality and class values. He therefore sees the necessity of preserving racial memory, the idea of the past as means of judging and ordering the present. Victorian and Edwardian period have offered peace an identity. Orwell believes that the middle class has given meaning to the human destiny.

In January 1941, Orwell has written a number of war time articles for a magazine. From August 1941 he has spent about two years as Talks Producer for the Indian Section of the B.B.C. Afterwards, he has used his B.B.C. experiences as the basis for the bureaucratic Ministry of Truth in his novel *Nineteen Eight-Four*. In February 1944 Orwell has completed his novel *Animal Farm*, and has been shocked when a leading publisher rejected it on political grounds. This novel is Orwell's most successful attempt to unify his political thought and artistic purpose. He condemns Russian Communism, the growth and decay of human psychology and revolutionary psychology. It is important to know that the pigs, Old Major, Snowball, and Napoleon are compared to Lenin, Trotsky, and Stalin. The *Animal Farm*'s enemies Pinch Field and Foxwoods, represent that forces of fascism and capitalism. *Animal Farm* is a good story and a devastating book.

Orwell himself has said about the novel that it has been the one in which he has tried, with full of consciousness of what he has been doing, to fuse political purpose into one whole. And the fusing is indeed complete. It is worth remembering, that right from the beginning this book has been taken by some simply as animals' story. Eventually the book has been brought out in 1945 by a different publisher. T.S. Eliot has praised this book for its literary merit. It is a satire against Russia, which has been in those days an ally of Britain. *Animal Farm* has proved to be a very successful book. Orwell has found himself financially well off for the first time in his life. His literary success is, however, marred by a personal tragedy. His wife Eileen, who has been in poor health throughout the war, has to undergo an operation and she dies at the operation-table. This has happened in February 1945.

In the winter of 1946, Orwell goes to the island of Jura in the Hebrides. His wife's death and his dislike for social life has made him to lead a lonely life. It is then, he has written his last book, *Nineteen Eighty-Four.* This has been published in 1949. But Orwell's health has been getting steadily worse. By the end of 1948, he has become seriously ill and has been hardly able to write anything. In September 1949 he goes back to London and enters a hospital. In October of the same year he gets married to Sonia Brownell. But his days are now numbered and he dies in January 1950.After the death of Orwell, his major essays are collected and has been published as *Shooting an Elephant, Such, Such Were joys*, *England Your England* and his *Collected Essays, Journalism and Letters* have appeared in four volumes. His works have been published in both standard and paperback editions in England and America, and have been translated into more than sixty languages.

Orwell's own bitter experiences, as a boy at St Cyprian's and Eton are described in *Such, Such Were the Joys* .It has appeared posthumously in 1952. Orwell's friend, Woodcock, has published the first series of essays about him in 1946 and 1948, before the publication of *Nineteen Eighty Four*. Cyril Connoly's *Enemies of Promise*, has been published in 1938 in which he makes fundamental criticism of Orwell's weakness: "the failure penetrate deeply into the rooted causes of injustices and lies against which he fights, and lack of any real constructive vision for the future of man"(118). Arthur Koestler in his article "A Rebel's Progress to George Orwell's Death" in *The Trail of the Dinosaur* pays an obituary where he has emphasised Orwell as a moral example and has said that, "the only writer of genius among the literature of social revolt between the two wars" (103).

Anthony Burgess (1917-1993) is one of the most prolific literary figures of the twentieth century. He has written many novels, plays, biographies, screenplays, criticism, and articles. John Anthony Burgess Wilson has been born on February 25, 1917, in

Manchester, England. He has studied violin and taught himself piano in addition to musical notation. Although he describes himself as a failed composer, his effort is not totally unsuccessful. He has created classical pieces and ratings for television, film, and theatre. Burgess's third symphony has been finished in Iowa Metropolis in 1975. In his lifetime, Burgess has composed musical works, concertos, and even operas. In the beginning, writing has only been a hobby for him. After he has realised his gift he turned it remunerative and a full time job. He has needed thirty five years of experience to get the concept for his novels.

Burgess has been raised in an Irish Catholic family and has attended Bishop Bilsborrow College and Xaverian University. He has lost his religion at Xaverian but has considered himself a lapsed Catholic. In 1940 after graduating from Manchester University with a degree in English literature, Burgess has entered the navy academic Corps from 1943 to 1946.He has worked as a training college lecturer in speech and drama on Gibraltar (1946-50). He has become a member of the principal Advisory Council for Adult Education within the Armed force, Birmingham during 1946- 1948. He has held many positions such as instructor of phonetics, drama, and literature for the Ministry of training, Preston, Lancashire, (1948-1950), and teacher of literature, phonetics, Spanish, and music, Banbury Grammar school, Oxfords hire (1950-1954).

In 1954 he has joined the British Colonial Service as a lecturer in English in Malaya. In 1957 he has become an academic officer and English language professional in Borneo. Burgess has started out his writing career as an observer of these politically and socially complex cultures. His first published novels, *Time for a Tiger* (1956), *Enemy inside the Blanket* (1958, and *Beds Inside the East* (1959) are set in Malaya. *Devil of a State* (1961) has been written in Borneo. He has taken the name Anthony Burgess because he has thought that his superiors would disapprove of his writing fiction. Anthony's Burgess's *Time for a Tiger* is a part of Burgess Malayan Trilogy. *The Long Day Wanes* is the first work of Burgess, published in 1956. The novel focuses on the unusual character of Victor Crabbe, a history teacher at an elite school, Malay. Burgess' *The Doctor is Sick* (1960) has been written in just six weeks after his return to Malaya from Burma. The title refers to the professor from Edwin Spindrift, a PhD degree holder. He leads an unhappy married life and has been sent to England from Burma. He has suffered from a mysterious brain tumour. The novel moves on with a dream sequence. The events in this novel are based on the experience which Burgess has felt in the Neurological Institute in London.

Anthony Burgess' *The Malaya Trilogy* is also published as the *Long Day Wanes*: *A Malayan Trilogy*. It is a comic novel based on the decolonisation of Malaya. The novel also explores the effects of the Malayan Emergency and also the British last life in south Asian Countries. The fourth exotic novel of Anthony Burgess' is *Devil of a State*. The novel is based on his experience when in Bander Seri Begawan, a Southeast Asian Sultanate on the island of Borneo. Anthony Burgess has published this novel under the pseudonym Josephine Kell in U.K. The author moves the novel with an indictment of British; he has seen the degradation of contemporary western education and culture.

In 1959 Burgess has returned to England and has been wrongly diagonised with a brain tumour. He has become a full time writer and has in fact completed, *The Doctor is Sick* (1960), *Inside Mr.Enderby* (1963), *The wanting Seed*(1962). In the dystopian novel *The Wanting Seed* Burgess expresses many social issues like discrimination of over population, religion and history. The most important portion of the novel deals with the damnation of war. Burgess's *Honey for the Bears* (1963) deals with the British antique dealers Paul Hussey and his American wife Belinda. They travel to Leningrad with a suitcase of dress to sell in the Soviet black market; on their trip Belinda develops a rash and she is taken to the hospital in Leningrad. Paul has various sexual adventures with both men and women and he looks for the freedom from a dissident composer. His goal is to write ten novels in order to provide an inheritance to his wife. However, in the website 'Your Dictionary' he has stated that, "I couldn't do it. I did produce five and a half though...And some of them are still around. But it was too much. I don't think anybody should do quite as much as that."

The five novels that Burgess finished at some point of his terminal year has proved a fitting assessment of the issues he would return to often all through his career. As soon as he has recovered from his misdiagnosed infection, Burgess has continued writing his novels. His *Nothing like the Sun: A Story of Shakespeare Love Life* is a fictional biography of William Shakespeare. The novel enlightens the so called relationships of Shakespeare with the notorious Elizabethan prostitute, Lucy Negro. The novel *A Vision of Battlements* by Anthony Burgess focuses on his experience during World War II in Gibraltar. He criticises the traditional notions of bottle heroism by imitating Aeneid with anti hero Richard Ennis. Burgess in his *A Vision of Settlements* explains "I was empty of music but itching to create. So I wrote this novel ….. to see if I could clear my head of the dead weight of Gibraltar" (7-8).

The novel *Enderby Outside* is the second volume in the series 'Enderly comic novels'. The novel begins with the protagonist who is under psychiatric care. He is working as a bartender in a hotel, London. He follows to renounce the creation of poetry as an adolescent preoccupation under the pseudonym Hogg, which happens to be the maiden name of his step mother. Burgess's *Napoleon Symphony: A Novel in Four Movements* (1974) is a fictional recreation of the life and world of Napoleon Bonaparte. The central theme of the novel is comic and also presents a detailed and revealing portrait of Arab and Muslim society under a Christian Western power. Burgess' most famous novel, but not his favourite, *A Clockwork Orange* (1962) is a satirical work detailing the violent exploits of a futuristic teenage gang and its Beethovan loving leader, Alex. The film version by Stanley Kubrick is so violent that it has been completely banned in Britain. Burgess has indeed dedicated this novel to Stanley Kubrick, who has directed the film.

The novella *The Clockwork Testament or Enderby End* is the third series of Burgess' novels. The sub title *Enderby's End* shows that this is the last book in this series. The novel is an account of Enderby's last day being alive. He has been working as a visiting professor of English literature and has composed long poems about St. Augustine and Pelagius. The novella moves on with Enderby's health issues and business. The novella ends with the death of Enderby. The novel *Beard's Roman Woman* by Anthony Burgess is set in Rome. The novel is based on the widowed Burgess in the 1960's.His wife Liana, is portrayed as Paola Lucrezia Belli in the novel. This novel is a companion piece to Burgess' next novel *Abba Abba.*

Anthony Burgess' twenty second novel *Abba Abba* focuses on the last month in the life of John Keats. The novel consists of two parts. Part one has various adventures of the poet meeting the Roman poet Giuseppe Gioacchino Belli and Pauline Bonaparte, sister of Napoleon; Part two consists of seventy sonnets by Belli, which are translated by Joseph Joachim Wilson, a descendant of Giovanni Gulielmi. The phrase Abba Abba refers to the words of Christon the cross. 'Abba' means father; Abba also refers to the enclosed rhyme, commonly used by Keats and Belli. The historical novel *Man of Nazareth* (1979) by Anthony Burgess is one of the trilogy novels of him, which deals with the biblical themes. This historical novel recalls the story of Jesus from his birth to his death.

During this time Burgess has succeeded in publishing many books such as *Shakespeare* (1970), and studies of James Joyce: *Re Joyce* (1965) and *Joysprick* (1973). Burgess has married twice. In 1968 his first wife dies due to the liver disease. Then he has married Liliana Macelli, a linguist. Owing to immoderate taxation and different life style in England they move to Malta. Burgess has visited the USA and has taught at the college of North Carolina. His comic style has softened his pessimism. The characters of his works have lurched from an outlandish journey to adventure. Burgess invented a dialect for *A Clockwork Orange*. A few books are considered intellectually greater than emotionally stimulating. Burgess' vitality and originality has been appreciated. He has published volumes of memoirs, *Little Wilson and Big God* (1987) and *You've Had Your Time* (1990). Both volumes have been commonly well-received by the critics. Some have complained that they spent an excessive amount of time on the summary idea. In his autobiography *Little Wilson and Big God,* Burgess has written:

> This novel was, is, about Brunei, which was renamed Naraka, Malay-Sanskrit for 'hell.' Little invention was needed to contrive a large cast of unbelievable characters and a number of interwoven plots. Though completed in 1958, the work was not published until 1961, for what it was worth it was made a choice of the book society. Heinemann, my publisher, was doubtful about publishing it: it might be libellous. I had to change the setting from Brunei to an East African one. Heinemann was right to be timorous. In early 1958, The Enemy in the Blanket appeared and at once provoked a libel suit. (143)

Although Burgess did not start writing till the age of thirty two, he has published his first novel at the age of thirty nine. He has been one of the busiest authours of his time. In addition to over twenty five novels, he has produced biographies, performs, screenplays, grievance, and articles. His translation of *Cyrano de Bergerac* has had a successful run on the Guthrie Theatre, Minneapolis, in 1971 and on Broadway in 1984. He has written Jesus of Nazareth, primarily based on his novel *Man of Nazareth* (1979) for television. Even when he has been sick he has published two works: *Dead Man in*

Deptford (1943) and *Byrne: A Novel* (1955). He is additionally a regular contributor to periodicals. Burgess has died on November 25, 1993 after a long struggle with cancer.

Phyllis Dorothy James White, the novelist who has written mystery novels is known as 'the Queen of crime'. P.D. James is considered to be one of the rare authors and also is compared with Agatha Christie, Dorothy L. Sayers and Margery Allingham. This consummate stylist has excelled in the detective genre. She has been given numerous awards for her eighteen crime novels, written within a span of half a century. Ralph C. Wood Easley who is a professor of Religion at Wake Forest university and author of the *Comedy of Redemption*(1998) feels that, "Unlike typical writers of thrillers, she fleshes out her characters with complex motives and particular features, and she fills in her setting with wondrous details"(277). She herself has informed the British critic and writer Julian Symons in1986 that her intention is to create a realistic cop as her hero, a dedicated and skilled police man. Adam Dalgliesh, the introspective Scotland Yard detective and published poet, functions as the hero in virtually all of her novels. He is something more than a police man, a complex and sensitive human being.

P.D. James, the pseudonym of Phyllis Dorothy James White, has been born on August 3, 1920 in Oxford, England. She is the oldest of three children. Her parents are Sidney Victor an Inland Revenue Official and Dorothy May James. Later, the family has moved to Cambridge, England, where Phyllis attended the Cambridge High School for girls. Phyllis has to leave the school at the age of sixteen because of financial problem in the family. She has got a job in tax office, where she has worked for three years. Later, she gets married to Ernest Connor Bantry White in 1941, who is an army doctor. They have two children. Even after marriage James does not lead a happy life; White returns from World War I seriously ill and in 1964 dies due to severe sickness.

Phyllis has decided to study hospital management and she has worked as a nurse at a hospital in England from 1949 to 1968. She is also the member of the Anglican and Lay Parton of the Prayer Book Society. She has been a government servant till 1979. While working in the hospital, she has started writing books. Her first novel is about an investigator Adam Dalgliesh of New Scotland Yard, the Headquarters of the British capital police service. All her novels focus on the criminal Justice system and the health service departments. Phyllis Dorothy has been a governor for the B.B.C. and Chairman of the literature Advisory Panel at both the Arts Council of England and the British Council. She has been awarded the OBE (Order of the British Empire) in 1983 and has beencreated a life Peer in 1991. She is the president of the Society of Author since 1997. She has received the following honorary degrees: Doctor of Letter from the University of Buckingham (1992), Herefordshire (1994), Glasgow (1995), Durham (1998), Portsmouth (1999), Doctor of Literature from the University of London (1993), Doctor of the University, Essex 1996. She is an Associate Fellow of Downing College, Cambridge 1986 and an Honorary Fellow, 2000. She has also been an Honorary Fellow at St. Hidas College, Oxford 1996 and Griston College Cambridge 2000.

P.D. James' *Shroud of a Nightingale* (1971) is one of the earlier works. As she has served as a nurse during the World War II, she is able to portray the life of a nurse from her personal experience. This novel deals with the student nurses Heather Pearce and Josephine Fallon, who have died of a perplexing situation in the Nightingale House. In order to inspect about the murder, Chief Superintendent Adam Dalgliesh is called to investigate the case. *An Unsuitable Job for a Woman* (1972),a crime novel of P.D. James, focuses on a female detective, Cordelia Gray, who is left with the struggle of a single-hand to investigate the death of her male partner. The society tells her that, this kind of job is not suitable for her because she is a woman. Overall, this detective novel brings out the gender, social, class prejudices about work, identities and women intelligence and strength.

P.D. James's *The Black Tower* (1975) is a detective novel which focuses on the two deaths at Toynton Grange; one is a suicide and the other is a heart attack. Later, two more deaths take place there. Adam Dangliesh arrives to investigate about the murder and finally he finds that 'Innocent Care Home' is the centre of drug smuggling operation. This leads to various deaths and murder in Toynton Grange. *Death of an Expert Witness* (1977), takes place in Chevisham, England, in the late twentieth century. In this novel, P.D. James highlights the expert witness Lorrimer, murder in his workplace, a forensic crime lab. Further, a middle-aged woman, Stella Mawson is also murdered by the same man, Dr.Kerrison. Meanwhile, the Scotland Yard Detective, Adam Dalgliesh using some clues finds out the motive that lies behind the murder of Lorrimer.

P.D. James' *Innocent Blood* (1980) is not strictly a detective novel like other novels. But, still it is a psychological thriller, which keeps the reader to know which way the protagonist will go, and what will be her future. The novel is about Philippa Palfrey who is adopted when she is eight into the wealthy family. In a nutshell, this story picturises, how genetics and environment, affect the child without knowing the truth. The detective novel *The Skull Beneath the Skin* (1982) is a novel where P.D. James brings in the female private detective Cordelia Gray for a second time. This novel spotlights the death of Clarissa Lisle, an actress who goes to an island in Dorset Coast with Sir George Ralston. In the island Clarissa has been receiving death threats in the form of quotations from the play in which she has played a main role. Before the performance of the play 'The Duchess of Malfi', Clarrisa is inhumanely murdered. The book talks about how Cordelia and the CID of Dorset solve the murder case successfully.

As discussed, dystopian novels examine the fate of an individual in a technologically advanced society. It is a fact that the world is progressing in a technological manner every second. It is not an exaggeration to say so because the advancement of science is like that. Initially, man has been thrilled to make new discoveries and the excitement of finding novel methods to do something, has been very fascinating and rather infectious. The new ways of technology have only eased man's way of life and so the desire to find more and more newer methods of advancement in all fields of life have ever been growing. Man has been rather very happy and joyful of his own findings and discoveries. But the pleasure in course of time has become gradually a matter of pride and it has in a way been led to sheer arrogance. In the beginning, man's scientific advancements has been meant purely for the benefit of humankind as a whole.

Unfortunately, the more and more of it has led to unpleasant and highly deporable walks of life. The good old proverb saying goes as, 'too much of anything is good for nothing'. Similarly, the surplus scientific innovations have indeed deprived mankind of valuable human emotions. There is no room for any sort of feelings and sentiments; only absence of culture and heritage. In short, human beings have to live in a society, which is totally devoid of humaneness. The democratic society may become under the total control of the supreme power which will only extend its arms of cruel clutches towards the people. This proposed thesis makes a modest attempt to prove that the novels taken up for study, namely, Huxley's *Brave New World*, Orwell's *Nineteen Eighty – Four*, Burgess' *A Clockwork Orange* and P.D. James' *The Children of Men* are dystopian novels for they project the fearsome future totalitarian society and display the salient features of the dystopian kind of novels. This study is based on humanistic theory.

BRAVE NEW WORLD

Aldous Huxley as a successful novelist and a prolific literary journalist has one of the most varied literary careers of his time. He has published three collections of poems and a book of short stories. A series of witty, sophisticated novels have indeed made him famous. His books are mostly satires of the English society of the 1920s. He believes that science is a weapon to destroy the human and political values. He has expressed this concern in the satirical novel *Brave New World* and this famous book describes a totalitarian society. Aldous Huxley and Orwell describe in their respective novels, *Brave New World* and *Nineteen Eighty-Four,* a very scary totalitarian society. Citizens have sacrificed their individuality and have forgotten about basic human rights. Harold Bloom says in his notes on Huxley's novel that it sees how "massive industrialization, coupled with severe economic depression and the rise of fascism formed Huxley's cautionary vision of the future" (14). Bloom also observes that *Brave New World* is still a vision of T.S. Eliot's *The Waste Land*, of a world without authentic belief and spiritual values (8). It disregards individual dignity and paves way for a sort of total submission, by nullifying individual freedom.

Totalitarian society literally worships science and has the least consideration for the aristocrats. According to Aldous Huxley, the plight of these people in the dark is only an outcome of the dictatorship fascination. The novelist is doubtful about the popular democracy. It advocates common capacities among unrefined and uncultured manual labourer. He deals with the menace of a dictator as the major theme of the *Brave New*

World. The title has been derived from Miranda's speech in Shakespeare's *The Tempest* in an ironic tone. *Brave New World* is in fact a dystopia, the exact opposite of Utopia. Lyman Tower Surgent is of the opinion that *Brave New World* is a warning. His foreword of *Island* suggests that a better alternative might be possible. Its ending implies that Huxley is not very hopeful that the people would change their ways.

Today *Brave New World* is considered to be an archetypical dystopian novel. It portrays a seemingly Utopian world. The critics are of the opinion that Huxley's ideas are rather provocative and fresh. His writing style is eloquent. He is appreciated for his analysis of post World War I English life. His promotion of humanistic values through literature is admired by critics. Margaret Cheney Dawson in *Huxley Turns Propagandist,* analyses this novel like this, "*Brave New World* is intended to be the Utopia to end Utopias, the burlesque of grandiose modern schemes for futurity. It is described by the publishers as "witty and wickedly satirical," but unless the substitution of Ford for God "Ford's in his flivver, all's well with the world"(221-22).

The novel opens in the building of the central London Hatchery. The conditioning centre happens to be the world state's motto 'community', 'identity' and 'stability'. The director explains to the students how mass production of hatcheries has been made possible by means of artificial insemination and fertilisation of eggs. Five types of beings are produced in the hatchery. The superior ones are called Alphas and Betas and the inferior ones are called Gammas, Deltas and Epsilons. The director describes with pride that,

> Alpha children wear grey. They work much harder than we do, because they're so frightfully clever. I'm really awfully glad I'm a Beta, because I don't work so hard. And then we are much better than the Gammas and Deltas. Gammas are stupid. They all wear green, and Delta children wear khaki. Oh no, I don't want to play with Delta children. And Epsilons are still worse. They're too stupid to be able. (22-23)

To shed more light on the characterisations, Peter Edgerly Firchow, an American critic and educator in his work, *The End of Utopia: A Study of Aldous Huxley's Brave New World* says that, "one of the chief problems, Huxley had with 'Brave New World' was with the characters"(154). According to this critic, "Character, after all, is shaped by suffering, and the new world state has abolished suffering in favour of a continuous, soma-stupefied, infantile happiness. In such an environment it is difficult to have characters who grow and develop and are alive"(154).

In the novel, The Director Mustapha Mond, one of the ten powerful world controllers gives a lecture to the students. He tells them that in his controlled society, there is no individual feeling as love. But there is communal spirit and casual promissory. Words like 'father' and 'mother' that denote personal relationships are prohibited. On the whole the disorderly life of the old world has been replaced by the orderly and planned life of the new world. Here people are happy and contented. Although in this new world, Bernard Marx, an alpha plus, is not satisfied with the system and his friend, Helmholtz Watson another alpha plus feels restless; they are made to feel hatred and bored by a fleshy girl called Lenina.

The novel portrays Bernard Marx, one of the alpha plus, as an intellectual as well as an individual, despite the nature of society they live in. Bernard feels alienated due to the physical defective made clear by the note in the novel. "Bernard had suffered all his life from the consciousness of being separate" (58). He is allowed to visit one of the few reservations, where people still live as savages. He goes to one such settlement in New Mexico with Lenina. She does not like the primitive life of the people there. They meet John, a slave born to Linda by the Director of Hatcheries. Linda now lives a promiscuous life on the reservation. Although John grows up to be an intelligent and self taught man, he remains a savage.

John, a savage in the novel, falls in love with Lenina with the permission of Mustapha Mond; Bernard takes John and his mother Linda, back to England. With his English knowledge, John proves to be a success in the London society. Lenina is a big believer in the hallucinogenic drug called soma and she thinks that it is a wonder drug. She sings silly chants such as "Put your arms around me...Hug me till you drug me, honey...Kiss me till I'm in a coma. Hug me honey, snuggly..."(170). Every citizen of the state takes the distributed hallucinogenic drugs soma to forget their dissatisfaction. It makes the takers to undergo a sort of surreal experience. Echoing the novel, "A holiday from reality whenever and come back without so much as a headache" (46).

The novel emphasises that the state of happiness in this new society is found through the drug soma. The slavish pleasure is focused, on an absolute good that, "one cubic centimeter cures ten gloomy sentiments" (46), and "a gramme is better than a damn" (47). Soma affects the people and makes them unable to feel a genuine emotion. They find it difficult to deal with even mild problems of everyday living: "soma had raised a quite impenetrable wall between the actual universe and their minds," (67), and this lack of touch with reality is strange and frightening. The drug Soma is an artificial substitute for actual experiences in life. According to critic Philo M Buck, Jr., in *Sight to the Blind: Aldous Huxley*, Soma which comes in medicinal pellets is cheaper and safer without any side effects of danger. The drug "Soma" and "Feelies" are the popular compensation for self-experience. Sometimes people feel craving for God, for danger, for excellence, and even for sin. Soma and Feelies which are safe and practicable come to their aid. As there is happiness in this sort of sensual pleasures, emotional attachments and personal relationships are unnecessary.

The people feel that there is a possibility for the achievement of a perfect world with this so called 'feel good' drugs. William W. Matter in his *Science Fiction Studies* analyses deeply into Huxley's motivations and thematic message. He says that Huxley "strongly opposed the belief that progress…would bring about a perfect world" and mentions the "questionable status of the individual" (147). He further quotes Huxley as, "rigid stability and unity…is stagnant and unproductive… Individuality does frequently disappear [and] wholesale industrialization creates men like machines" (148). Moreover, in his evaluation of soma, the central idea of escape resurfaces. He says, that "[w]hen pleasure and escape become unavoidable goals…the individual lives in a nightmarish ideal society that cannot allow him the right to be unhappy" (148), and that "soma is evil because it is used for escape (149). The role of soma is generally agreed by analysts of *Brave New World.* They have focused in detail on its negative implication for the individual in society and on its function as a sort of escape route from reality. Lenina becomes attached towards John but because of her loose morals, he rejects her. In the beginning, the new world attracts John but finally he is disgusted with it and revolts against its laws.

The world controller Mustapha Mond summons Bernard, Helmholtz and John after their rebellion. Bernard and Helmholtz are exiled to the Falkland Island, but John is detained and Mond has a philosophical discussion with him. He tells John that in the brave new world, there is no room for art, literature and religion. Bringing psychoanalytic theory to further analyse this, one finds out that, Freudian Criticism deals with a character's outward behaviour. It may conflict with inner desires with undiscovered inner desires, in dreams. To find out the meaning of dreams is essential. According to psychoanalytic theory, a person's sub conscious desires are revealed in his dreams. Social rules seem to control a person's expressions. There are no social rules in dreams. The secret desires have been stamped in the subconscious mind that goes unchecked in sleep.

John is not convinced by Mond's explanation. He argues in favour of the primitive impulses and human feelings. He advocates for individual freedom and a well ordered society, free from science. The god, mother, father, Shakespeare, and conventional morality are important. He does not want to be an object of scientific experimentation. He is physically attracted towards Lenina but his mind rejects her. As he cannot bear this, he goes to the light house on the coast of survey to live as a hermit. John returns to the life of a primitive savage. Whenever he remembers his lust for Lenina he whips himself. The news of his eccentric behaviour spreads far and wide and people from various places come to see that whipping of him. Lenina also comes to see this scene. John gets angry with her and he whips her to death instead of whipping himself. When people come there next, they see that he has hanged himself in the light house. He has committed suicide because he cannot adjust himself to the way of life the new world.

Aldous Huxley's *Brave New World* gets its title from Shakespeare's *The Tempest* in which the heroine, Miranda, sees for the first time a good number of people including her dream- man, Ferdinand. She says in ecstasy "O Wonderful"! How many godly creatures are there, how beauteous mankind is! O Brave New World. That has such people in it"? (113). But Huxley's *Brave New World* does not have godly creatures and beauteous mankind. Therefore the title itself is used satirically. As Shakespeare's *The Tempest* is also a utopian of the dramatist's imagination, the title itself speaks of anti-utopian chamber of Huxley's *Brave New World.*

Thomas More has presented in his *Utopia* a blue print of a happy society with suitable distribution of wealth and all other necessities of life including food, clothes and shelters. He has envisaged a social order in which everybody has to work in the farms, but nobody is exploited. In a world of Thomas More, Utopia is a classless society. It is said that Thomas More has been the first communist of the world with a vision of a classless society, whereas the social order in *Brave New World* has several classes of

Alphas, Beta, Gammas, Deltas, and Epsilons. Henry Hazlitt's *What's Wrong with Utopia* describes in detail the rigid caste system in Huxley's novel:

> The Alphas represent the highest intellectual class, from which all the directors are recruited; they are selected from the finest chromosomes, and developed in their bottles under optimum chemical conditions. The classless graduate down through Betas, Gammas, Deltas, and finally Epsilons, who do most menial work, and are even purposely stunted in growth by a shortage of oxygen in their incubator bottles. The purpose of the caste system is social stability. (204)

Each of these classes has its allotted work according to the conditional hierarchy. Naturally it is Anti-Utopian or dystopian novel. Thomas and Hudson in their *The History of an Idea* assert that, the Garden of Eden is the key model for the original Western, Judaea in Christian Utopian tradition, and expulsion from it would possibly imply that subsequent human life in itself is dystopian.

Brave New World has been first published in 1932. It is classified as a dystopian novel or anti utopian along with Zamyatin's *We* (1920-21), Koestler's *Darkness at Noon* (1940) and Orwell's *Nineteen Eighty Four* (1949). After the 1932 publication of *Brave New World* Huxley is despaired about the real world significance of one of his novel's principle themes. David Bradshaw in his, "Introduction" to *The Hidden Huxley* remarks,

> About 99.5% of the entire population of the planet are as stupid and philistine...as the great masses of the English. The important thing, it seems to me, is not to attack the 99.5%...but to try to see that the 0.5%

> survives, keep its quality up to the highest possible level, and, if possible, dominates the rest. The imbecility of the 99.5% is appalling but after all, what else can you expect. (xx)

Huxley has been deeply dejected and disillusioned by the uncongenial effect of the World War I. In a letter to his brother Julian in August 1918, he predicts that the war would accelerate American domination over the world. There is a general opinion against Americans that has been reflected in Fanny Trollope's *Domestic Manner of the Americans*, Dickens', *American Notes* and Alexis de Taequeville's *Democracy in America*. America is the present model for Huxley's vision of the future. It emerges even more clearly from his essay entitled, "The Outlook for America Culture, Some Reflection in a Machine Age," published in 1927 where Huxley observes, "speculating on the American Future, future of civilized man. The world to come, America universalized, would be ruined by the "standardization of ideas"; "imbecility" will "flourish and vulgarity cover the earth…" (265). As far as it is concerned, one of the most ominous portents of the American way of life is that it embraces a large class of the people who,

> Do not want to be cultured, are not interested in the higher life. For these people existence on the lower, animal levels is perfectly satisfactory. Given food, drink, the company of their fellows, sexual enjoyment, and plenty of noisy distractions from without, they are happy. (148)

Aldous Huxley also feels that America is vulgar and freakish as he has anticipated when he visited America in 1926. He has said in the final section of *Jesting*

Pilate about execration of the gimcrack movies, blank-faced 'pneumatic' flapper's barbarous jazz and unrelenting pep which Huxley has found in Los Angeles. Huxley declares dolefully in no uncertain terms that, the future of America is the future of the world. According to him America, is fast getting industrialised, represented by Ford. The industrial workers have become machine like, devoid of human sensibilities and emotions. Huxley's *Selected Letter* describes American society as "Materially the nearest approach to utopia yet seen on our planet" (189). The Wall Street crash of 1929 has severe consequence on industries. The increased unemployment and economic problems have grown more and more acute and out of proportion. As the crisis deepened, Huxley's pessimism has increased in the same proportion. National government is to deal with emergency and the abandonment of the gold standard has marked the worksheet of English history between the wars. Huxley has to postpone his second visit to America shortly after his disappointment. He has felt like many of his contemporaries to renounce parliamentary democracy and to submit to the rule by men.

Huxley has felt in the beginning that Utopia is indistinguishable from Ford factory but the events of 1931 have changed his views. When Huxley has been writing *Brave New World*, he asserts that stability is the primal and ultimate need if civilization has to survive the present crisis. According to him they should increase the output to meet the economic problems. Naturally he has a high opinion about people running the industries. His Mustapha Mond, the resident controller for Western Europe is named after Alfred Mond, chairman of 'Imperial Chemical Industries Ltd', the vast plant which is utilised by Huxley only a little before writing *Brave New World.* Huxley's interest in agencies which is the science of controlled proceeding to increase the occurrence of heritable characteristics is revealed in his *Proper Studies* (1927). Bokanovsky process, Podsnap's technique, New Pavlovian conditioning, and Hypnopaedia described in *Brave New World* are the parts of Eugenic process.

The public remembers eugenics as limited to the atrocities committed in the name of Nazi racial hygiene. It is difficult to accept the novel's bizarre scenario. It is an expression of particular Anglo American eugenic concerns and polices. Huxley asserts that intellectuals are from all points on the political spectrum and not just conservatives or fascists. They are drawn to eugenics as a progressive, technocratic means of improving the health and fitness of populations. All this background proceeds to dystopian chambers, though *Brave New World* is so problematic for Huxley, as he is not writing a satire a prophecy or a blue print. He answers to a question that he is neither with the savage nor with the ideal of conditioned stability. Clyde Chittyin in his book *Eugenics , Race and Intelligence in Education,* says that "I believe some mean between the two is both desirable and possible and must be our objective"(38).

Huxley has given a detailed description of the process of keeping control on breeding and conditioning. In *Brave New World* an outsider, with some knowledge of the world prior to Bokonovsky process is given the role of a protagonist. According to critics Reber and Reber in *The Penguin Dictionary of Psychology,* people consider individual identity as "a person's essential, continuous self, the internal, subjective concept of oneself as an individual"(338). The notion of oneself as an individual is replacing with, "the set of behavioral or personal characteristics by which an individual is recognizable as a member of a group" (338). But the terms he has used, make it clear that he does not mean human population.

Words like hatcheries, conditioning, fertilizing, and incubators, are suggestive of using methods for selective breeding. The human embryos can he developed in a test tube as this novel describes. Even in the modern days cloning is in elementary stage and cloning of human beings has not been possible nor is found desirable. Even Huxley does not seem to have any fancy for this process. He has created The Savage, Bernard Marx and Helmholtz who revolt against the very concept of selective breeding. Conditioning has made the people machine like; unable to think anything beyond what is put in their heads. They have become persons without imagination and aspiration. Soma is given to them to induce a sense of satisfaction with what they are getting. Even the feelies are meant to divert the minds from hard realities of life. They have happiness but it is available in a limited sense. When the physical needs are well supplied and free, it has kept everyone free from family worries in the past, present and even in future.

Scientific invention has made it possible to keep people safe from genetic problems. Thus, people are kept free from worries and ambitions and the society is satisfied and is kept safe from instability in all respects. It is a total transformation of men into tame and docile animals. Religion, science, and philosophy are kept out of bounds. People should think of new dimensions of human personality. Mustapha Mond, being the highest authority in the Western Europe, remarks in the novel:

> The world's stable now. People are happy; they get what they want, and they never want what they can't get. They're well off; they're safe; they're never ill; they're not afraid of death; they're blissfully ignorant of passion and old age; they're plagued with no mothers or fathers; they've got no wives, or children, or lovers to feel strongly about; they're so conditioned that they practically can't help behaving as they ought to behave. (193-194)

The question is at what expense, this citizen gets this blissful life. The traditional method of women giving birth is gone to the winds. They are the manufactured products of Bokanovsky process. R.T. Oerton, in his essay "The End of the Beginning", provides more information about Bokanovsky Process,

> In *Brave New World,* some of the fertilised ova were subjected to Bokanovsky's Process to which the eggs responded by budding to produce "identical twins but not in piddling twos and threes as in the old viviparous days, when eggs would sometimes accidentally divide; actually by dozens, by scores at a time.(48)

During his discussion with the savage, Mustapha Mond declares, that the plays of Shakespeare are prescribed in the world state for no reason but that, it is old and beautiful. He is afraid that everything beautiful will cause ripples in the otherwise placid waters of conditioned society. God is beautiful. So God has been replaced by Ford. They swear by Ford, and he speaks about religion in terms of condemnation, very close to those of blasphemy. He rejects the religious view, presented by religions in the following words,

> We are not our own any more than what we possess is our own. We did not make ourselves; we cannot be supreme over ourselves. We are not our own masters. We are God's property. Is it not our happiness thus to view the matter? Is it any happiness or any comfort, to consider that we are our own? It may be thought so by the young and prosperous. (190)

Denying this age old belief, Huxley asserts that independence is not made for men since it is not safe and will never carry people to the end. He declares that it was a great thing. Echoing the words of Huxley from the novel,

> To be without the irksomeness of continual acknowledgment, continual prayer, continual reference of what they do to the will of another. But as time goes on, they, as all men, will find that independence was not made for man-who in an unnatural state- will do for a while, but will not carry us on safely to the end. (205)

Huxley is not prepared to accept the religious theory that people are here to do God's will as, Milton believes , men should "stand and wait" for His orders. Mustapha Mond thinks that people remember God in perversity, and when they become old and infirm, but not in their youth. He is totally convinced that people turn towards God only during their 'testing times'. As long as they are happy, young and energetic, they seem to enjoy life without the slightest inclination towards the Almighty. But Huxley feels that men turn towards God mostly when they are in their advanced years. The reason is nothing else other than the fear of death and also a dreadful thought of life after death. Huxley in his own words from the novel,

> It is negation of truth; It is the fear of death and of what comes after death that makes men turn to religion as they advance in years. But my own experience has given me the conviction that, quite apart from any such terrors or imaginings, the religious sentiment tends to develop as we grow older. (205)

It is misleading that man remembers God not in love but in fear of death. The examples of saints prove the falsity of such a statement or rather immoral. It is based on such principles as "everyone belongs to everyone" which in turn has sanctioned and forced, prostitution in the society. Mustapha Mond supports indulgence in youthful desires, which he thinks are necessary for enjoyment of life, forgetting that enjoyment has other nuances, too. There is no reason why people should not be pegged down to lower forms of enjoyment. Mustapha Mond finally gives his clinching opinion like this: "God isn't compatible with machinery and scientific medicine and universal happiness. You must make your choice. Our civilization has chosen machinery and medicine and happiness. That's why I have to keep these books locked up in the safe" (207). That has silenced the opposite side when they differed from Mond's views. Mustapha Mond defines philosophy, "As the finding of bad reason for what one believes by instinct. As if one believed anything by instinct! One believes things because one has been conditioned to believe them. Finding bad reasons for what one believes for other bad reasons-that's philosophy" (207).

The savage counters this view and argues that one tends to think about God naturally, not due to conditioning, but when one meditates in solitude. But Mustapha Mond makes it clear that nobody in the World States is allowed to think in solitude. It is clear that Mustapha Mond's government has taken statutory steps to stop people from thinking in solitude lest people should turn to god in a natural way. But the Savage quotes Edgar of *King Lear* who says to the mortally wounded Edmund that "The gods are just, and of our pleasant vices make instruments to plague us" (207), to punish men for their vices. But the controller says that Edmund will not be punished for his vices in the changed scenario. He adds that Edmund will have the pleasure in the present conditions to sit in pneumatic chair with his arms round a girl's waist, sucking away at his sex-hormone chewing gum. "The wheel is come full circle" (208), in a different sense. Man would not be punished for his misdeeds. He implies that the old view God dispenses justice is not true anymore. But the savage holding to his conviction asks whether Edmund sitting in the pneumatic chair is not as heavily punished, as Edmund is wounded and bleeding to death. The punishment he gets is in the form of moral degradation. In his opinion it is not a bit less when he sat in pneumatic chair. The controller then puts an end to this issue saying that they are looking at the issue from different viewpoints. The controller's opinion is that nothing will degrade a man, if he does not believe in God's justice.

The controller goes to the extent of saying that values like self-denial or chastity are meaningless in the modern indulgence. He points out "Industrial civilization is only possible when there's no self-denial. Self-indulgence up to the very limits imposed by hygiene and economics. Otherwise the wheels stop turning" (209). In the opinion of Huxley, the demand of the industrial civilisation has increased the consumption of goods. Quoting from the text, "Degrade him from what position? As a happy, hard-working, goods- consuming citizen he's perfect"(208). He dismisses the idea of chastity, since he thinks that it evokes passion and neurasthenia which is an exhausted condition of nerves or low state of health and which can result in instability. Obviously a man in passion and in health will have no reason to complain against the social order.

Mustapha Mond is antagonistic to the spirit of nobility and heroism. It will induce people to transgress the limits to human endeavours and aspirations. A heroic man is to rise above the set limits. He further adds that heroism and nobility can be noticed in the War, in divided allegiances or in resistance of temptations. But the conditioned society has no place for them. The savage is of the view that struggle for a minimum prize is necessary to keep people in spirit. He refers to the story of the boy, who braved the biting of the flies and mosquitoes all over his body while hoeing the garden of a girl to win her love. The Controller however does not appreciate the spirit of romance in the story. He points out that in the civilised world, one can get the girl without hoeing the garden. But the Savage is not happy with this emotionless society. He is thinking of his mother Linda all the while. In his emotions for his mother he overrules the controller's argument saying "What you need," the Savage went on, "is something with tears for a change. Nothing costs enough here" (211), and with this end in view he declares,

> I'm claiming the right to be unhappy. "Not to mention the right to grow old and ugly and impotent; the right to have syphilis and cancer; the right to have too little to eat; the right to be lousy; the right to live in constant apprehension of what may happen to- morrow; the right to catch typhoid; the right to be tortured by unspeakable pains of every kind. (212)

The Savage values freedom and independence more than anything else. The controller does not believe the passion for life of love and emotion. Mustapha Mond has given strong arguments in favour of Bokanovsky process. But the savage has brow beaten him on several points. Mustapha Mond thinks that there is no necessity of God, religion, philosophy, etc. This will not convince any normal human being, much less the savage. He holds the view that uncontrolled and unconditioned society is better, having several social evils and health hazards. Mustapha Mond, representing the culture of the World State, is defeated and brow beaten in discussion on all the aspects of the social order of *Brave New World.* It can, therefore, be safely concluded that Huxley has written this novel to belittle the industrial civilisation that is growing in America. His novel therefore, is dystopian and a satire upon the social order.

The novelis set in the year A.F. 632, that is 632 years after the advent of 'the American magnate', Henry Ford. His successful 'model T' is the first automobile manufactured on a mass production method. Ford has replaced God in *Brave New World.* They celebrate 'Ford's Day' and swear 'by our Ford'. The World State motto is community, identity and stability and not liberty, equality and fraternity. The world stability means control on population explosion and also ideas which are inconsistent with the state policies. It is through biological engineering and exhaustive conditioning that population is maintained at the desirable level. The Director explains "The Predestinators send in their figures to the Fertilizers who give them embryo they ask for" (7). The embryos are 'hatched' in the Hatcheries. The Bokanovsky's process is one of the major instruments of social stability. The director declares with confidence, "If we could bokanovskify indefinitely the whole problem would be solved" (5). The words such as 'Fertliser' and 'Hatchery 'clearly indicate that intricate mechanism in limited numbers of manufacturing cars. People are manufactured according to the demand.

The Bokanovsky process controls not only number but also the qualities of men. There are Alphas-plus, Alphas, Gammas, Epsilons and so on and so forth. These classes of men are divided into a hierarchy. Oxygen is supplied below par to Epsilon Embryos, and Epsilons do not have human intelligence. The miners, acetate silk spinners and steel workers are conditioned to thrive on heat. Thus, people are conditioned for specified nature of work. Conditioning aims at making people like their inescapable social destiny. They are predestined for their roles in the society. The lessons are rubbed in with mild electric shocks. Some of them are treated in such a way at an early stage that may produce hatred of books and flowers. Gammas, Deltas, even Epsilons have been conditioned to like flowers to make them want to go into the country at every available opportunity, because consumption is economic necessity.

Hynopaedia is another method to give lessons while the child is asleep. Bernard, a perfect conformist mockingly quotes the sleep technology as "civilization is sterilization" (94). He is fully aware of the fact that Directors are great liars and create stories to keep society in line. There is a case of Reuben Rabinovitch who has the chance to hear a broadcast programme from London while he is asleep. When little Reuben wakes up, he repeats word by word, a long lecture by George Bernard Shaw, who is speaking about his own genius. This example prompts hypnopaedic method of giving lessons. Embryos are given lessons in elementary sex and elementary class consciousness. The minds that judge and desire and decide are made up of suggestions given by the state. Thus, everything and every person is under the State Control. Nobody can think beyond what he or she is conditioned for.

The general principle inculcated to stop people having their own predilections even in matters related to life partners, is "Every one belongs to everyone else" (34). No man and woman can live together for a long time. When Lenina confides to Fanny that she has been with Henry Foster for four months, Fanny warns her.

> It's such horribly bad form to go on and on like this with one man. At forty, or thirty-five, it wouldn't be so bad. But at *your* age, Lenina! No, it really won't do. And you know how strongly the D.H.C. objects to anything intense or long-drawn. Four months of Henry Foster, without having another man-why, he'd be furious if he knew… (34-35)

Thus, people are denied to have their individual likes and dislikes, so that they accept what comes their way or what is given to them. Ford or Freud is the first to reveal appalling dangers of family life. Condemning the life in pre-conditioning days, it is observed, "The world was full of fathers-was therefore full of misery; full of mothers-therefore of every kind of perversion from sadism to chastity; full of brothers, sisters, uncles, aunts-full of madness and suicide"(33).

Families are considered dangerous to social stability. Nobody is allowed to have leisure. Everybody has to remain busy. An idle man can think of another way of life. Quoting from the book "Work, play-at sixty our powers and tastes are what they were at seventeen. Old men in the bad old days used to renounce, retire, take to religion, spend their time reading, thinking-*thinking!"* (45). Thinking now is, therefore, an anathema and Soma becomes an unavoidable necessity. It rather helps,

> The old men work, the old men copulate, the old men have no time, no leisure from pleasure, not a moment to sit down and think - or if ever by some unlucky chance such a crevice of time should yawn in the solid substance of their distractions, there is always *soma*, delicious *soma*, half a gramme for a half-holiday, a gramme for a week-end, two grammes for a trip to the gorgeous East, three for a dark eternity on the moon; returning whence they find themselves on the other side of the crevice, safe on the solid ground of daily labour and distraction, scampering from feely to feely, from girl to pneumatic girl, from Electromagnetic Golf course to…(47)

Man is the product of the society, not vice versa. No individual can think for himself. Aldous Huxley has predicted in one of his letters to his brother that the American domination over the world will increase as an inevitable consequence of the World War I. The same and, similar views are expressed by other writers. Dickens, for example has expressed similar views in his *American Notes*. Huxley has said on a number of occasions that the future of America is the future of the world. He foretells that America is approaching nearer to Utopia. The World State in *Brave New World* contains huge skyscrapers, dollar economy, cult of youth, feeling, gender hormone chewing gum, etc. When Huxley has visited America in 1926, he has found every bit as vulgar as he has anticipated. He goes to Durham coal field where he is appalled by mass unemployment. Therefore, he writes like several contemporaries of his, that the time has come to renounce parliamentary democracy and submit to rule by men. It will be men who will compel people to do and suffer what a national foresight demands.

In an answer to a journalist, Huxley in 1935 replies that his sympathies are neither with Savage's aspiration nor with the ideals of conditioned society. He thinks that some means between the two, both desirable and possible and that must be the objective. He is not clear whether his *Brave New World* is a satire, a prophesy or a blue print. The title of the novel suggests that it is a satire since the savage uses it in utter disgust whereas Shakespeare has written these words to describe a pleasant surprise and admiration of Miranda for the people she sees, all of a sudden at such a later stage of her life. Again the words such as 'Hatchery', 'Fertilizer' are suggestive not of men, but of animals.

The unmistakable impressions given by Bokanovsky process show that men are conditioned to become spineless fellows, following the commands of the state, without having any personal views on any matter. Bokanovsky process produces slaves, who are given Soma to keep them happy in their respective conditions. 'Soma' and 'Feelies' compensate for the instinctive striving for unique self expression. They are safe and practicable. Each individual will feel safe and happy instead of having personal dissatisfaction with his environment. Sometimes they feel, the craving for god, for danger, for excellence, even for sin, when sin is unique and personal, says Buck, principles such as 'everyone belongs to everyone else' are meant to create animals, doing sex without consideration for the character of man or woman one copulates with. The novelist seems to suggest that industrial civilisation that Ford represents will create workers of several classes, and most of them will depend on drugs after an excruciating day full of work.

Huxley describes the society which is both real and satirically denunciating. Nobody ever wishes to have a society of self-negating workers. Bernard Marx, Helmholtz Watson and the Savage are created obviously to present a better class of persons who demand freedom of thought. It certainly sounds ridiculous when Mustapha Mond speaks against *The Holy Bible*, and Shakespeare. He says, "A whole collection of pornographic old books. God in the safe and Ford on the shelves" (204). He suggests that religion and God are irrelevant in the Fordian concept of the society. Ford stands for stability of the society, for materialistic pleasure and happiness whereas God stands for spiritual joy. In support of his view that Ford stands for happiness, he says that man turns to God when he is old and sick, not when he is young and strong. Mustapha Mond points out that,

> They say that it is the fear of death and of what comes after death that makes men turn to religion as they advance in years. But my own experience has given me the conviction that, quite apart from any such terrors or imaginings, the religious sentiment tends to develop as we grow older; to develop because, as the passions grow calm, as the fancy and sensibilities are less excited and less excitable. (205)

Mustapha Mond thinks that Shakespeare is also out dated for the simple reason that he upholds higher values of life and sets the great store by the human relationship, the values and passion of love above all other things of life. There is no place for human relationship and emotions, attached with them in the World State. Mustapha Mond disapproves *Othello* and other tragedies of Shakespeare mainly because "our world is not the same as Othello's world. You can't make flivvers without steel-and you can't make tragedies without social instability. The world's stable now" (193). And *Romeo-Juliet* is discarded because there is no sense in anybody being made for any particular boy or girl in the World State. These bizarre and grotesque ideas obviously stand against the natural order of things, and are satirical in spirit.

But it can be said that Huxley articulates against the fast disintegrating society due to industrial culture. As the industrial civilisation is spreading its tentacles, family ties have become the first and greatest casualty. There is no father, mother, sister, or brother left as these relationships in the World State are banned. Again, religious or moral values have been thrown to the winds. Happiness of the self is the main consideration as good food clothing, houses and feelies are the only necessities in the World State. As God is of no concern to anybody in the modern life, beauty and truth are meaningless words. Mustapha Mond argues,

> Universal happiness keeps the wheels steadily turning; truth and beauty can't. And, of course, whenever the masses seized political power, then it was happiness rather than truth and beauty that mattered. Still, in spite of everything, unrestricted scientific research was still permitted. (201)

Happiness is the chief concern of the people in modern times.

The *Brave New World* has been an enigma to the soldiers. Huxley himself cannot say whether he has meant this novel to be a satire, or a prophesy or a blue print. So the scholars have found it difficult to dissect. M. Buck in his essay "Sight to the Blind: Aldous Huxley" in *Directions in Contemporary Literature* claims that Huxley's novel is a satire. According to him,

> Thomas More's *Utopia* is a satire, in the form of a novel, a description of our lives as they will be in the none too distant future. It will happen if the present obsession persists for standardisation, according to the sciences eugenics and psychology, as well as economic and mechanics. Thus, though it purports to be a look into the future, it is much more an assessment of the present. For example, the little song in which the

> scientifically processed inhabitants of the world find a substitute for the emotion of art:
>
> Hug me till you drug me, honey;
> Kiss me till I'm in a Soma:
> Hug me, honey, snugly bunny,
> Love's as good as soma
>
> Any night on the radio, or from the dance orchestra, drug like this is poured out by crooners. It is not a caricature of the theme song- it is Hollywood. And people like it. (173)

Sometimes, it appears to confirm D.H Lawrence's observation about the present industrial culture. When D.H Lawrence visited New Mexico, he says that his experiences have liberated him from the great era of material and mechanical development as Huxley's Savage has done in his case. The Savage is certainly a better man than any other man in the civilised world. According to Firchow Peter. E in *The End of Utopia: A Study of Huxley's Brave New World,* "The individual is no longer isolated, but he is no longer isolated because he is no longer an individual is to be isolated, is to be unhappy; to be integrated is to be "happy" but happy in an inhuman fashion"(154).

John has emotions and regards for his mother, whereas the words like mother, father, etc are not used in the World State. When Linda is sent to the hospital to die, the Savage has rushed to see her. But the nurse at the hospital is surprised to see him worried, since nobody in the World State is supposed to worry for any relatives. They are not supposed to have any emotions. Tears welled up behind the eyelids of the Savage as he recalls the rhymes she used to sing to him in his childhood days and the stories of the other world she has narrated to him.

The Savage stands in frozen silence and goes down on his knees when Linda has breathed her last. Linda's death has terribly shaken him. *Brave New World* can be construed as a tribute to D.H Lawrence but Huxley is not in sympathy with regressive attitude. He has not showered success upon the Savage and his two revolutionary companions. On the contrary all the three are punished for their revolt. Bertrand Marx named after famous Karl Marx is rather brought to disgrace as he apologises and blames his two companions for inciting him to treason. The two of them are sent to the island while the third, decides to live in anonymity at a deserted place. Later he commits suicide.

Huxley, therefore, is neither with Mustapha Mond nor with the revolutionaries. Again it is just not possible to read the Savage Reservation as antithesis of inhuman World State because lives of Linda and her son, John, are by all accounts miserable and abominable. Following the principle 'Everyone belongs to everyone else', she has made herself a prostitute and has received beatings from women whose men have visited her. John has dreadful experiences of life. Just like light and darkness cannot co-exist, society and individualism cannot coexist with the other. Disaster will follow if one tries to combine them together. In *Brave New World*, towards the end of the novel John the Savage is mentally crushed. He bursts out in a voice of despair, "Oh, Linda, forgive me. Forgive me, God. I'm bad. I'm wicked. I am ...No, no, you strumpet"(223). His frustration and weakened mental state results in his suicide and society's victory over individuals. But Huxley does not approve of the life, governed and controlled through Bokanovsky process either. In fact he is unable to prepare a blue print for an ideal organisation of the society. The best he can do and he has done is to present all the aspects of life as he has seen and visited.

Huxley cannot make it clear in *Brave New World* as to what kind of society he would prefer. Therefore, he explains his position in the foreword to *Brave New World* written in 1946. He accepts that he has committed a mistake,

> To prob over the literary shortcomings of twenty years ago, to attempt to patch a faulty work into the perfection it missed at its execution, to spend one's middle age in trying to mend the artistic sins committed and bequeathed by that different person who was oneself in youth- all this surely vain and futile ….. However, it seems worthwhile at least to mention the most serious defect in the story. (xxxix - xxxx)

The first serious defect, according to him is that he has offered only two alternatives to the Savage, an insane Utopia, or the life of a primitive in one Indian village, which is more human in some respects but hardly less queer and abnormal. He admits that when he has written the book he has found it amusing that man is given a choice between sanity and lunacy. After fourteen years of interaction with the eminent critics, he finds that man is taken as a 'sad symptom of the failure of an intellectual in time of crisis'. He is convinced that sanity can be achieved.

Huxley has mentioned in his "Foreword" that he is sure, if he is to write the book again, he will offer the Savage "Between the Utopian and the primitive horns of dilemma would lie the possibility of sanity – a possibility already actualised, to some extent in a community of exiles and refugees from the *Brave New World*, living within the border of the Reservation"(1). In his new scheme of things he will present science and technology as the promise for future prosperity and happiness of man. Religion will be used for "conscious and intelligent pursuit of man's Final End, the unities of knowledge of immanent Tao or Logos, the transcendent Godhead or Brahman" (1). To find a golden principle for ultimate happiness of man, he will recommend a kind of high utilitarianism, in which the greatest happiness principle would be secondary to the final end principle.

In his newly conceived plot, he does not bring the Savage directly to Utopia until he has learnt about the nature of 'society composed of freely cooperating individuals devoted to the pursuit of sanity'. Thus, he believes that *Brave New World* possesses an artistic and philosophical completeness. Huxley regrets that he has not mentioned the use of the nuclear energy for power, although it has been a popular topic of conversation for years before the book is written. He is sure that the release of atomic energy can blow one to bits. Huxley however, has believed that the real revolution is to be achieved not in the external world but in the souls of human beings. He is sure that Robespierre's political revolution and Sade's revolution will make a revolution of sexual anarchy by stability. He does not think that atomic power will bring revolution. He is also afraid that atomic power will bring destruction of mankind in spite of precautions which are being taken.

Huxley has visualised that America will, in course of time, make people to love servitude. He is very much sure of that for in his 'Forward' to the novel he says,

> The most important Manhattan Projects of the future will be vast government - sponsored inquiries into what the politicians and the participating scientists will call 'the problem of happiness'- in other words, the problem of making people love their servitude. (xlvi)

The love of servitude will come, when problem of permanent security is solved. According to Huxley, love of servitude can come only as a result of deep personal revolution in human minds and bodies through discoveries and inventions. The first method to bring revolution, is through conditioning; the second method is to bring social economics hierarchy; the third is to find harmless and pleasure giving substitute of alcohol and other narcotics and the fourth is to get full proof system of eugenics (science of producing healthy off springs). He admits that the standardisation of the human beings has been pushed to fantastic extremes, yet he declares that nobody knows what will happen in A.F.600.

Huxley believes that his prediction of brave new world has started appearing to be true. The sexual promiscuity as described in the novel does not appear to be distant. He observes that in certain American cities the number of divorces is equal to the number of marriages: "In a few years, no doubt, will marriage licences be sold like dog licences, good for a period of twelve months, with no law against changing dogs; or keeping more than one animal at a time" (52). Then, the influence of dope and movies and the radio would help the subjects to reconcile to servitude. Huxley's *Brave New World* and Orwell's *Nineteen Eighty Four* have been proved to be true in their foresight.

Huxley is describing a future of physical health and also of the right of the individual not to be made to suffer more, the right to differ, to succeed, to have one's reservation. *Brave New World* is scientifically efficient, biologically equipped, and psychologically informed than the societies of the Wellsian. Orwellian tradition which is far more tolerant. Huxley's explorations and convictions have increased. He becomes far more hopeful about the human spirit's capacity to grow. However, he hopes that the men in power in the democracies will cease to drift. He is not a defeatist, an escapist, or a deserter. Edward Hobb declares like this in his *The Subversion of Drama in Huxey's Brave New World,* "Brave New World thus, against the odds, and contrary to the opinions of several critics, a work in which form and content are artfully combined"(91).

Sometimes Utopia, with its ups and downs in various types of situations seems to be a good idea. It results in many broken hearts, deaths, and humiliation in *Brave New World.* It might be Huxley's warning to the current society about what could happen in the near future. It is high time for the people to take a stand for what they believe in. It just goes to show one that it is difficult for a perfect world to exist. Huxley's satirical point in this novel is that if the present continues to progress as it is progressing now, and then the inevitable result must be a Brave New World, says Peter E .Firchow. According, to a critic, a proper understanding of the novel is very important. To quote the critic

Peter E .Firchow "to be extraordinary or to be an individual is to be criminal; thinking or feeling deeply are punishable offences" (457). He further adds that,

> (in)spite of all the efforts of technology and psychology directed at reducing man to an automaton, some semblance of humanity and individuality still survive even if only accidentally. In this sense *Brave New World* cannot be seen as pessimistic novel; the hope for a continuation of humanity is not altogether extinguished. (457)

The critics in general consider Huxley's dystopia to be a mockery of scientific and social progress of the early twentieth century. The government and industry have been dreaming of this progress. It is that the progress should be within the desired limitations of being beneficial to the individual and to the society in the larger scale. It should not pave way for the society to rule over the individuals in the most harmful manner. The individuals make up the society and the society is for the individual. Huxley is also proud to see the advanced mode of technology and science. But at the same time he is very much aware of the wrong and dangerous path that science is treading upon. The novelist wants to create awareness among the people of the forthcoming precarious society of science and hence has written this dystopian novel. By writing this, he is very much sure that at least he has made his readers realise that such a dangerous totalitarian society is not an imaginary event but can happen in reality if not taken care of. In fact, Huxley feels the bit of contentment in himself, for having written this dystopian novel for it indirectly serves the mankind by enlightening them of the forthcoming huge avalanche of the totalitarian society.

NINETEEN EIGHTY-FOUR

Eric Arthur Blair, an English novelist and social critic, with a chosen pen name George Orwell is an unique combination of a middle class intellectual and working class reformer. An unmistakable autobiographical element runs through most of his novels and essays. It provides a sense of conviction immediately. His description of living in poverty in the *A Clergyman's Daughter* can be taken for example. This novel is an attack on social injustice. It exposes those miseries and hypocrisies of the poor middle class background to the near starvation of the slum dweller. *Homage to Catalonia* (1938), a non fiction work is based on a brief carrier of a soldier during the Spanish Civil War. His disillusionment with a Loyalist can be clearly seen in this novel. The threat of the World War II is reflected in his novel *Coming Up For Air*. Using George Bowling, an insurance clerk as his mouth piece, Orwell mirrors the suburban frustration and political concerns. These thoughts are occupied in the mind of Orwell thoroughly.

The publication of the novel *Nineteen Eighty-Four* has won him name and fame. The novel is a frightening portrait of a totalitarian society where love is punished, privacy is lost and truth is distorted. He uses a grim tone to differentiate this book from his other novel, *Animal Farm* which is a satire on the communist government of the Soviet Union under Stalin. *Nineteen Eighty-Four* is written in the custom of the utopian novel, and is perhaps best defined as a dystopian novel, literally the opposite of a perfect society. Orwell's novel shares a communal identity with Aldous Huxley's *Brave New World* and more significantly Eugene Zamiatin's *We*, both of which Orwell has read prior to the publication of this novel. Although different in structural context, Orwell's novel is comparable in thematic design and development and it is noticeably dissimilar to that of Huxley and Zamiatin. They create futuristic societies, totally unlike the present in which they have been written.

Orwell deliberately has constructed a remarkably realistic and recognisable future. Zamiatin's *We* is an early fictional narrative criticising, the then emerging Soviet Russia. It is extremely similar to *Nineteen Eighty-Four* and this novel has clearly influenced Orwell's perception of the totalitarian state. It has confirmed much of his political and creative ideology. Zamiatin's novel can certainly be credited in providing Orwell with thematic direction, character analysis, and conceivably the most effective vehicle, with which to communicate his artistic message. Stability is the greatest threat to any totalitarian rule. In connection to Hitler's Germany and Stalin's Soviet Union, Hannah Arendt in *The Origins of Totalitarianism* argues that:

> To a totalitarian movement, both dangers are equally deadly: a development toward absolutism would put an end to the movement's interior drive, and a development toward nationalism and frustrate its exterior expansion, without which the movement cannot survive. Stability stops the totalitarian movement, it offers a chance of a normal life, and there is no reason for global expansion. (389)

Nineteen Eighty-Four is George Orwell's a reliably grim vision of a dystopian future. The author considers it as a warning more than an insight. In this novel he talks about the dangers of conformity, mental coercion, and verbal deception and, he also retains their validity and relevance. Orwell's careful use of clear, comprehensible language makes the unfamiliar world of *Nineteen Eighty-Four* understandable to the readers. His theme of personal individuality and human emotion, particularly love is trying to establish them amidst the pressure of the modern industrial state. So it has a perennial appeal to the people. This is Orwell's dystopian novel about the future. It is a warning to the world, a very vivid presentation of the terror that could occur in the near future. The totalitarian power postures cruelty in this novel.

The novel is sub divided into three parts. The first part introduces the hero, Winston Smith, to the readers. A terrifying picture of the community in which the hero lives is given. It introduces the handful of characters who serve the plot, including Julia, with whom Winston will fall in love. It informs about the state with the telescreen installed in every living room, through which secret police constantly supervise the words, gestures, expressions, and thoughts of all members of the party. The readers come across Newspeak, the language devised by the party to prevent independent thinking. The Big Brother's face who governs everything is to be seen everywhere on posters. Doublethink is the formula for hundred percent hypocrisy; the three slogans are 'War is Peace', 'Freedom is Slavery', and 'Ignorance is Strength'. The party's technique of obliterating the past events is done in the party's interests. The political system which prevails is Ingosc which is congruent to English socialism. This is a deliberate attack on socialism and socialist parties in general; it is not the socialism of equality and human brotherhood in which Orwell himself believes, but the socialism of Marxism which promotes communism.

The second part of the novel describes the plot which is a very simple one. Winston falls in love with a black haired girl, Julia. This is in itself an act of rebellion on the part of both of them. Echoing from the novel, "The sexual act, successfully performed, was rebellion. Desire was thought crime" (62). A description of their love making follows and these passages alone contain a lyrical, sensuous quality utterly lacking elsewhere in the book. Winston and Julia, already rebels, now become more active in their plot against the party. They contact O'Brien whom they believe to be a fellow rebel. O'Brien gives them a copy of a book supposedly written by Emmanuel Goldstein, the enemy of the party. Winston reads the book, and it is a typical Orwellism that Julia falls asleep while Winston reads it aloud to her. Women are not intelligent in the world of Orwell.

Goldstein's book is called, 'The Principles of Oligarchical Collectivism' and the novel has many pages of quotations from it. It contains a logical and coherent account from the world situations. Orwell is expected it to develop in the coming twenty five years or so. Later, it turns out to be that the book is written actually by the party itself. Orwell's use of an old nursery rhyme is noteworthy. The rhyme begins: "Oranges and Lemons, said the bells of St. Clément's". It ends with the words "And here comes a chopper to chop off your head" (202). Orwell's use of a simple rhyme to achieve in due course an effect of extreme horror is a brilliant and typical Orwellism which places him as a craftsman in the front rank of the English novelists.

The third part of the novel narrates the torture and the breakdown of Winston Smith, following upon his arrest in bed with Julia by the secret police. This part is overwhelming in its picture of a thorough extermination of all human feelings in a human being. Orwell here gives a full rein to his sadism and its attendant masochism. One can see them rising to their heights in the scene where Winston, is threatened by hungry rats which will eat into his face and he is compelled to betray all that is noble in a man. At the end of it, he is a broken man ready for reeducation as a willing follower of Ingsoc. His plight at this stage is the necessary prelude in Oceania, he being shot for his thought crime. In Ingsoc there are no martyrs, but only broken men wishing to die for the good of their country. It is almost intolerable to read the third part of the novel which, even more than the rest of the book, smells of death, decay, dirt, diabolism and despair. O'Brien is the grand inquisitor, and he leaves Winston.

The world, as imagined by Orwell, consists of three States namely Oceania, Eurasia, and Eastasia which are perpetually at war with each other. From time to time these states keep changing sides and the people have no clear idea at any moment of who are their allies or their enemies. The object of these continous wars is to use up the excessive productiveness of machinery and yet, contradictorily, to get control of rare raw materials or cheap native labour. Another important attraction of war is that it enables the new governing class, which is modeled on the Stalinists, to keep down the standard of living and nullify the intelligence of the masses. 'War is Peace' is the party slogan and it indicates that war is not itself necessary but that the collective oligarchy can operate securely only on a war-footing.

Orwell's novel is concerned with the moral corruption of absolute political power. London lies decaying like an old cabbage with the remains of its nineteenth century buildings, but high above the street's tower are the four main Ministries of Ingsoc: the Ministry of Truth, whose function is to propagate the lies which suit the Party; the Ministry of Plenty whose function is to ensure a continuous scarcity of most of the commodities, and the Ministry of Peace whose function is to conduct war. The Ministry of Love is the one which is windowless and surrounded by barbed wire and machine-guns and where political prisoners are either executed or reformed by the Party officials. Richard Rorty in *Contingency, Irony, and Solidarity* says,

> (Orwell) sketched an alternative scenario, one which led in the wrong direction. He convinced us that there was a perfectly good chance that the same developments which had made human equality technically possible … make endless slavery possible. (175)

A rebellious man is seized and taken into the Ministry of Love from where he will eventually come out fully converted, incapable of any private life and without any memories of the past. In this totalitarian State, private memory and the sexual impulse are the two deadly sins. In every home, a telescreen is fitted from which party propaganda continually pours out and on which the pictures of Big Brother, the leader, and Goldstein, the traitor and the enemy, often appear. Also by this device the, Thought Police keep an endless watch over "thought-crime" and can observe the people day and night. 'Thought crime' in general terms means the tendency to lead a secret private life. A frown, a smile, a shadow on the face, a sigh may betray the citizens who have forgotten for a moment the art of "reality control" or in the official language (Newspeak) "doublethink".

Winston Smith's doubts begin when by chance there comes into his hand a complete piece of evidence of the lies told by the State. The doubts propel him to action. He buys a notebook and starts writing a diary which is forbidden by the regulations. He tries to define "doublethink" as thus: "To know and not to know, to be conscious of complete truthfulness while telling carefully constructed lies, to hold simultaneously two opinions which cancelled out, knowing them to be contradictory and believing in both of them"(31). The appendix of the novel describes the operation of the official language of Oceania as devised to meet the official needs of Ingsoc or English Socialism. The language is divided into the 'A vocabulary' which is "the words needed for the business of everyday life" (242); The B vocabulary consists of "words which had been deliberately constructed for political purposes: words, that is to say, which not only has in every case a political implication, but are intended to impose a desirable mental attitude upon the person using them"(244); The C vocabulary is nothing but the "scientific and technical terms"(249).

Newspeak, the new language being evolved by the Party, is the natural offspring of doublethink. This is how Syme, the Party philologist, explains the aim of the new language to Winston: "You think, I dare say, that our chief job is inventing new words. But not a bit of it! We are destroying word— scores of them"(46). The aim of Newspeak is to narrow the range of thought and to remove from literature all those elements which could pollute the minds of the members of the Party. The time will come when the official slogans will not be required simply because, "there will be no thought as we understand it now"(48).

In *Nineteen Eighty-Four*, the world is organised into three great political entities. All of them profess the same philosophy; yet, despite their agreement, or because of it, the three super states are always at war with each other. Two of them are always allied against one, but all see to it that the balance of power is kept by means of sudden, treacherous shifts of alliance. Although it is the ultimate aim of each to dominate the world, the immediate aim is the endless war without victory and without defeat. War is regarded as a sign of the health of the State. According to the official slogan, 'War is Peace' and perpetual war is the best means of maintaining absolute perpetual power. It is also the most efficient method of consuming the production of the factories on which the economy of the State is based. The only alternative method is to distribute the goods among the population. But this has a clear danger. The life of pleasure is contrary to the health of the State. It stimulates the senses and thus encourages the illusion of individuality. It creates personal desires and may thus lead to personal thought and action.

All past despotic rulers have claimed some general good in their desire to rule and have claimed to be philosopher-kings or priest-kings or scientist-kings, with an announced programme of benevolence. The rulers of Oceania in this novel, however, know that power in its pure form has for its true end, nothing but itself. And they know also that the proof of power lies in the suffering and the pain which the rulers can inflict upon others. The exposition of the mystique of power is the heart and essence of this novel. That mystique is implicit throughout the narrative, and explicit in extracts from Goldstein's book called *The Theory and Practice of Oligarchical Collectivism.* It is Winston Smith, the sad hero of the story, who is compelled to accept the theory of O'Brien by being subjected to a sort of physiological torture and discourse. He has violated the Party code by believing that sexuality is a source of pleasure, that personal loyalty is something fine, and that two and two always make four. At length, Winston is made to believe that two plus two makes five.

Orwell's theory of power is developed brilliantly and sufficiently. According to Jean Jacques Courtine's article published in *Substance:* "Totalitarian power has a real stake in language and aims to dominate it. This is the warning given by Orwell in 1984 with his invention of Newspeak"(69-70). The usage of political language results in the loss of critical thoughts. The politicians wantonly make use of unnecessary and complicated words. They do not prefer clean and concise language. The social system which demands it is described with marvelous circumstantialities the three divisions of the population namely, Inner Party, Outer Party, and Proles. The complete watch over the citizens by the thought police; the total negation of the personal life; the directed emotions of hatred and patriotism and the children who spy on their parents and the total destruction of culture is picturised. Orwell is particularly successful in his exposition of the official mode of thought, 'doublethink', which gives a man "the power of holding two contradictory beliefs in one's mind simultaneously, and accepting both of them" (194).

This novel is certainly, and to a large extent, an attack on Soviet communism. But Orwell does not have only Soviet communism in mind when he has written this book. What he wants to say is that Russia, with its socialist revolution, has developed into a police State. But the threat of the Russian type of totalitarianism exists almost everywhere today. Orwell's book has therefore a wider significance than it is generally thought. Arthur Koestler has rightly commented in *Darkness at Noon* that Orwell's novel,

> … c learly refers to real life system, the Soviet Communication of The Leader (Lenin) and Number One (Stalin). Orwell, in contrast, always maintains a general conception of a totalitarian system which is not tied to a specific country or ideology. As O'Brien makes clear; there were the German Nazis and the Russian Communists.
>
> The Russians presented heresy more cruelly than the Inquisition had done…" (96)

Nineteen Eighty-Four is undoubtedly a political novel. Orwell has, in an article, spoken of a tension which he has felt between the public and the private lives. That tension is the heart of this novel. When Winston thinks, "Nothing was your own except the few cubic centimeters inside your skull" (24), he is expressing the basis on which

Orwell's whole morality rests. Orwell here expresses his belief, that to be human is to be private and to have a personal identity that is inward and inviolable. Winton's rebellion against the Party in this novel is an attempt to preserve that small area of privacy; to think, and to feel as himself, as a private individual, without interference or encroachment. Authority in a totalitarian State tries to destroy personal identity entirely by whatever means possible. It is significant that the only sciences which have made any considerable progress by the year 1984 are the science of invading privacy; and the science of torture. Both these sciences are a means of controlling and altering identity. Personal identity is an important consideration.

There are also certain other important considerations. For instance, the past is unchangeable, that truth is objective, words have fixed meanings, and that love is possible. *Nineteen Eighty-Four* is a dreadful book, because in it every one of these propositions is denied. These ideas have been fundamental to Western liberal culture since the time of the Renaissance. All western institutions, sciences, humane studies, arts, human relationships depend on these ideas. But in the world of *Nineteen Eight-Four*, these are unwanted. In this world men are expected to live without a past, without truth, without a clear language, and even without love. It is partly with this feeling that a great period of human culture has ended and this makes the novel so profoundly depressing. The critic Joseph Winters in his article published in *Journal for Cultured and Religious Theory* says

> It would be cynical to say that a plan for a better world is manifested in history and unites it… No universal history leads from savagery to

> humanitarianism, but there is one leading from the slingshot to the megaton bomb. It ends in the total menace which organized mankind poses to organized men… History is the unity of continuity and discontinuity. Society stays alive, not despite its antagonism, but by means of it. (320)

The values of the novel are thus political values, and Orwell's respect for them places him in a political tradition which is the liberal tradition of western culture. Orwell is a great believer in decency, liberty, and justice. He is also a believer in what may be called 'ordinariness'. Orwell has chosen, as he says, 'the form of a naturalistic novel' for the writing of *Nineteen Eighty-Four*, in order that the action might be rooted in a setting of everyday reality. He has invented his hero, a man without exceptional qualities, so that the whole novel might be filled with a sense of probable existence. Thus, Winston's need for truth and love are ordinary needs, such as one might feel under a totalitarian system, and his hope is in the ordinary people. Winston believes in the myth of the proletariat, as seen when he enters into a conversation with an old man in the public. He discovers the truth about the past, and when looking at the washer-woman, he thinks that "the proles were immortal" (200). This too is a political statement; this faith is the survival of ordinary people, beyond systems. The action of the novel, however, does nothing to confirm this faith; it simply exists as faith, as it does in Orwell's mind.

The hero, Winston Smith, in the novel is a citizen of England which has become Airstrip One, a province of a super-State known as Oceania. He lives in London on which fall twenty or thirty rocket-bombs a week, where there are rotting houses, empty bomb-sites, electricity cuts, a chronic shortage of one commodity after another, cigarettes that fall to pieces, evil-tasting food, and so on. This dinginess, this barrenness and listlessness seem even more truly characteristic of modern life than its cruelty and insecurity. Quoting from the text, "The ideal set up by the Party was something huge, terrible and glittering. The reality was decaying, dingy cities where underfed people shuffled to and fro in leaky shoes. He seemed to see a vision of London, vast and ruinous, city of a million dustbins" (67).

There are regulation lunches in the community centres, where the attendance is fully checked; the Junior Anti-Sex League is designed to destroy the erotic attachment between people, which might set up private loyalties; the Youth League and the Spies, whose members have been issued with ear-trumpets so that they can more easily listen to their parents' conversations. The children have been changed into horrible, ungovernable savages, adoring everything connected with the Party. In the words of Orwell from the novel,

> It was almost normal for people over thirty to be frightened of their own children. And with good reason, for hardly a week passed in which The *Times* did not carry a paragraph describing how some eavesdropping little sneak—'child hero' was the phrase generally used overhears some compromising remark and denounced its parents to the Thought police. (22)

The party apparatus of the government is to be found everywhere. Above all, it exists in Newspeak the official language, the sole aim of which is the narrowing of the range of thought by the destruction of vocabulary, and in the telescreens of the thought police which can receive and transmit simultaneously. It is a technical device which destroys all private life. Nicholas Lemann has rightly remarked in *The Limits of Language* "To Orwell, the connection between the English language and politics was that the debasement of the latter requires the corruption of the former"(31). An attention should be paid to the language. As it is a tool for the regime it affects the society. One does not know when one is being watched. Possibly everybody is watched all the time and in the words of Orwell from the novel, "You had to live in the assumption that every sound you made was overheard, and, except in darkness, every movement scrutinized"(2).

The above account is that of the culture of a perverted English Socialism, known as Ingsoc, administered from the Ministries of Truth, Peace, Plenty and Love. It is the last that is really frightening for it is not only windowless but is also surrounded by a maze of barbed wire and machine-gun nests: "Even the streets leading up to be armed with jointed truncheons"(4). Oceania is governed by the elite 'Inner Party', consisting of two per cent of the population which rules on the basis of its slogans: War is Peace, Freedom is Slavery and Ignorance is Strength. The Party has two major problems: the conquest of an earth and the prevention of independent thought; and science exists only in so far as it helps to achieve these. Its fundamental principle, based on the idea that nothing exists except through human consciousness, is that of reality-control a lunatic dislocation of the mind that in Newspeak is called “doublethink”.

Doublethink gives way to the erasure of memory. Winston cannot remember the origins of Big Brother, the party, or the philosophy ‘Ingsoc’: “just once in his whole life he has held in his hands unmistakable documentary proof of the falsification of a historical fact. And on that occasion …”(32). And there Winston’s recollection is disrupted by the exercise instructress on the telescreen. ‘Doublethink’ means the power of holding two contradictory beliefs in one’s mind simultaneously, and accepting both of them. Doublethink lies at the very heart of Ingsoc, since the essential act of the Party is to use conscious deception, while retaining the firmness of purpose that goes with complete honesty. The necessity is to believe and tell deliberate lies. Inconvenient facts are forgotten but drawn back whenever necessary. The existence of objective reality is denied. Ultimately it is by means of doublethink that the Party has been able to arrest the course of history. It is arrested by continually altering it. In fact there is no past but only a kind of continuous present in which the Party is always right. The slogan is: “Who controls the present controls the past” (224).

The complete Party man is happy in a world where there are no friends but only comrades, where a love-affair is impossible and the lunatic credulity which the Party needed in its members, be kept at the right pitch, except by bottling down some powerful instinct and using it as a driving force. A party member has no spare time and is never alone except when in bed. To do anything requiring solitude is dangerous; it suggests that forbidden individualism or eccentricity which is described by the Newspeak word "own life". The greatest evil is "thought crime", and the greatest virtue is to be "good thankful." In Newspeak there is even the concept of "face crime" which is to wear an improper expression on one's face. For example, one should only look incredulous, when a victory is announced. There is also the concept of 'crime stop', the faculty of stopping short as though by instinct, at the threshold of any dangerous thought.

The twin poles of this society are Big Brother who is considered to be infallible, omnipotent, immortal, and omnipresent through his gigantic photographs and Goldstein who is the enemy of the People the defiler of Party purity, and the author of a terrible book called *The Theory and Practice of Oligarchical Collectivism*. The world against which Orwell warns is the world which is supposed to have emerged after the atomic war of 1950 and after ten more years of conflict revolution and counter revolution which thenensued. Russia by then has absorbed the whole of Europe and created the super-State of Eurasia; the U.S.A. has welded America and Great Britain into the super-state of Oceania; the third super-State has arisen later under the name of Eastasia. Each of these three super-states has been subjected to a totalitarian system, known respectively as Neo-Bolshevism, Ingsoc, and Death-Worship. Fredric Warburg in *George Orwell: The Critical Heritage* points out,

> Two of the principal super states will obviously be the Anglo-American world and Eurasia … (The Anglo-Americans) will have to find a new name for themselves. The name suggested in *Nineteen Eighty Four* is of course Ingsoc, but in practice a wide range of choices is open. (247)

Their political philosophies are indistinguishable. Yet each regards the other with fanatical hatred and they are in a constant state of war.

The doctrines and structure of Ignsoc, the system governing Oceania in general and Airstrip One or Great Britain in particular are described in detail. At the summit of the pyramid stands Big Brother, the mystical personification of State power, whose identity and even existence are in doubt. Below him comes the Inner Party, the Brains of the whole organism, who control the Outer Party or functional class. The remaining eighty-five per cent of the population are known as the proles, who enjoy no political or social rights, and are relegated to the status of animals.

The aim of the Inner Party is to seek power entirely for its own sake: not wealth, or luxury or long happiness, only power, pure power. For this purpose it is necessary for the Inner Party to eradicate all individual thoughts or feelings. The thought Police or Thinkpolis aided by a device known as the telescreen by which they are able to watch the movements, listen to the conversations, and even note the expression on the face of every individual citizen. A momentary flicker of doubt upon the features of an individual would be noted as a “facecrime”. An individual, guilty of such an outrage would be ‘vaporized’ and his existence is removed from the records so that he would become an ‘unperson’ that is, a non-existent person. Not only that, the whole of the past and the current history is distorted and falsified. The very language is curtailed in order to eliminate independent thinking. Sex is discouraged; the family is disrupted and the children are taught to spy and hate. By such methods the individual is compelled to abandon his personality; a dark uniformity is created; a listless apathy is infused; and a condition of acute boredom is enforced. Orwell has succeeded in impressing upon this awful twilight of the mind.

The picture of the society in *Nineteen Eighty-Four* has an awful plausibility. In some ways, life in the year 1984 as visualised in this novel does not differ very much from the life one lives today. The pannikin of pinkish-grey stew, the hunk of bread and a cube of cheese, the mug of milk less Victory coffee with its accompanying saccharine tablet are that kind of meal which is not unfamiliar to many of them. It can recognise, too, the Victory gin which has "a sickly, oily smell, as of Chinese rice-spirit"(4) and which gives to those who drink it "the sensation of being hit on the back of the head with a rubber club"(4). By creating a world in which the proles still have their sentimental songs and their beer, and the privileged consume their Victory gin, Orwell involves the reader most skillfully and uncomfortably in his story. He succeeds in getting one's belief in the fantasy of thought-domination that occupies the foreground of his book.

The objective of the State is to achieve complete thought-control and to cancel the past utterly from the minds as well as from the records. A telescreen, which receives and transmits simultaneously, is fitted into the residence of every member of the Party. The telescreen can be dimmed but not turned off, so that there is no way of telling when the Thought Police have plugged in on any individual wire. To this end, also a new language has been invented, called "Newspeak", which is slowly displacing the traditional English or "Oldspeak". The chief function of Newspeak is to make a heretical thought literally unthinkable. A heretical thought is one which deviates from the principles of Ingsoc or English Socialism. The object of Newspeak is, in other words, to restrict the range of thinking. The end-objective of the members of the Inner Party who control Oceania is expressed in the Newspeak world "doublethink" which means,

> To know and not to know, to be conscious of complete truthfulness while telling carefully constructed lies, to hold simultaneously two opinions which cancelled out, knowing them to be contradictory and believing in both of them, to use logic against logic, to repudiate morality while laying claim to it, to guardian of democracy, to forget whatever it was necessary to forget, then to draw it back into memory again at the moment when it was needed, and then promptly to forget it again: and above all, to apply the same process to the process itself.(31)

No other book has succeeded so completely in rendering the essential quality of totalitarianism as *Nineteen Eighty-Four*. This novel is, however, limited in its scope. It does not investigate the origins of the totalitarian State, nor the laws of its economy, nor the prospect for its survival. This novel simply evokes the tone of life in a totalitarian society. Not being a realistic novel, it can treat Oceania as an extreme example, one that might never actually exist but which throws much light on the nature of the political systems that do exist. The book shows Orwell's firm belief that in a totalitarian world man's life is deprived of its dynamic possibilities. Oceanic society may evolve through certain stages of economic development, but the life of its members is static. Such a life is specified and is in measured quantity; it can neither rise to tragedy nor tumble to comedy. The human personality has here been obliterated. Man has become a function of a process which he is never allowed to understand or control.

Of course, there have been totalitarian societies in the past. But in most of them it has been possible to find an oasis of freedom, because none of them has the resources to enforce total obedience. But the totalitarianism of Oceania, permits no such freedom at all; it offers a total solution to the problems of the twentieth century, and that means a total distortion of what might be a solution. But Orwell has thought, it to be worthwhile to visualise the extremity of totalitarianism. This totalitarian State assumes that if given the modern technology, complete political control, the means of terror, and contempt for moral tradition then anything is possible. Anything can be done with men, anything with their minds, anything with history, and anything with words. Reality is no longer something to be acknowledged or experienced. It is fabricated according to the need and the will of the State, sometimes in anticipation of the future and sometimes as retrospective improvement upon the past.

One of the most touching scenes in this novel is that in which Winston Smith, trying to discover what life has been like before the reign of Big Brother, talks to an old prole in a bar. The conversation is unsatisfactory to Winston because the aged worker can remember only fragments of disconnected facts and is unable to generalise from his memories. But the scene itself is a fine bit of dramatic action. It indicates the totalitarian society. It destroys not only the past through the obliteration of objective records, but also the memory of the past through a disintegration of the individual consciousness. This aged prole remembers that the beer has been better before the time of Big Brother. But he cannot really understand Winston's question, "Do you feel that you have more freedom now than you had in those days?"(82). To understand such a question requires a degree of social continuity which Oceania is gradually destroying.

The destruction of social memory becomes a major task in Oceania, where any embarrassing piece of paper is thrown into the fire. Orwell is similarly acute in noticing the relationship between the totalitarian State and what passes for culture. Novels are produced by machines; the State anticipates all needs, from cleansed versions of Byron to pornographic magazines. That vast modern industry, which is known as "popular culture" has in Oceania become an important function of the state. Meanwhile the language is stripped of words that suggest refinements of attitude or gradations of sensibility. Steven Blackmore has said in *Language and Ideology in Orwell's 1984* that,

> Orwell's great insight was to see that any ideological assault on human nature is intimately connected to the assault on human language…Moreover, he saw that the essential textuality of human time and history is precarious in a world where language and texts are destroyed. (355-6)

At the same time, Oceania seeks to extinguish all feelings and emotions. Winston Smith recalls how precious the feeling of his mother towards him and his little sister used to be. But Oceania has no need of such affection. Winston simply cannot help recollecting the feeling of maternal tenderness of his mother. Reproducing from the text, "When the last of the chocolate was gone, his mother had clasped the child in her arms. It was no use, it changed nothing, it did not produce more chocolates, it did not avert the child's death or her own; but it seemed natural to her to do it" (134).

Orwell's extensive reading and experience has prepared him for the rise of totalitarianism in the world and the uses that the dictators would make of their power. For example, the Italians have been under Mussolini since 1919. In the 1930s, however, the Soviet Union and Germany has to began develop in dangerous ways which reminds Orwell, of the hierarchical absolutism of the Roman Catholic Church. He notices particularly their pyramidal structure and the emergence of a new ruling caste to direct it. Such political systems, he thinks, may become permanent and universal. He believes that the attempt to establish the dictatorship of the proletariat would end in a rule by a select class of people, enforcing their will through terrorism. The Russian Communists have thus, in Orwell's view, developed into a permanent ruling caste or oligarchy; a caste system has joined to a collectivist economy. It is what he has also seen taking shape in Germany.

Thus, Orwell finds that the two regimes, namely, communism in Soviet Russia and fascism in Germany, having started from opposite ends, have rapidly evolved towards the same system as a form of oligarchical collectivism. The phrase "oligarchical collectivism" is first used by Orwell for these two totalitarian States in 1940. Thus eight years before the publication of *Nineteen Eighty-Four,* Orwell has summarised the structure of the totalitarian States as it later appeared in his novel. It is noteworthy that the book written by Goldstein in this novel is called 'The Theory and Practice of

Oligarchical Collectivism'. Several causes have sharpened Orwell's conception of what the totalitarian State might be like. The worst possibility, he has imagined is that the great powers will arm themselves with atomic weapons which they would be afraid of using. Orwell has summed up the power-structure that is to appear in the novel. It would mean the division of the world among two or three vast super-States, which are unable to conquer one another and also at the same time unable to be overthrown by any internal rebellion. In all probability their structure would be hierarchic with a semi-divine caste at the top and an outright slavery at the bottom.

Orwell has written that, such a slave State, has every chance of becoming permanent. As early as 1939 Orwell has felt that men's minds might be so manipulated as to guarantee their total submission for all time. He has then written *Orwell and Politics* where he says, "…The terrifying things about modern dictatorships are that they are something entirely unprecedented. Their end cannot be foreseen. In the past every tyranny was sooner or later overthrown, or at least resisted because of nature which as a matter of course desired liberty..." (315). One cannot be certain, at all, that human nature is constant. It may be possible to produce a breed of men who do not wish for liberty.

The main theme of *Nineteen Eighty-Four* is thought-control in general and control over the past in particular. In this field, the vividness of Orwell's imagination is remarkable. At the first level, thought-control is exercised by two-way television sets in every room by means of which the Thought Police can see and listen to every citizen at any time, day or night. At the next level the government introduces a new language called "Newspeak", the object of which is to make it impossible for anyone to express any thought opposed to the principles of Ingsoc. The replacement of present-day English by Newspeak is intended to destroy human reason by linguistic means. To the ordinary reader of this novel, Orwell's tour de force of the imagination is extremely effective in giving him an idea of the extent to which language, truth, and logic are inter-dependent. One chief object of Newspeak is to cut impossible ideas:

> All words grouping themselves round the concepts of liberty and equality, for instance, were contained in the single world "crimethink" while all words grouping themselves round the concept of objectivity and rationalism were contained in the single word "Oldthink". (246)

Orwell has provided a detailed and learned linguistic Appendix to the novel dealing with the problems presented by this enterprise. This Appendix in many respects is much more alarming than the melodramatic incidents of the third part of the novel. The members of the Party have also to be provided with a philosophy. This need is met by "doublethink", a philosophy which enables its followers to believe a proposition at one level and its opposite at a deeper level. Timothy Garton Ash's in his essay "Politics and the English Language" published in *The Guardian* sums up the central Orwellian argument that the corruption of language is an essential part of oppressive or exploitative politics. He further says, that the defence of the indefensible is sustained, by a battery of euphemisms, verbal false limbs, prefabricated phrases, and all the other paraphernalia of deceit that he pinpoints and parodies.

Winston has begun to deviate from the Party code, though only in his thoughts. He knows that such deviations will lead to his death under torture; but he cannot wholly control his thoughts. His downfall is natural. The girls of the Outer Party are subjected to an intensely puritanical education which is intended to make them incapable of any pleasure in the sexual act. Sexual intercourse between married partners is permitted but only so long as it is joyless. All other sexual intercourse is punishable with death. Winston has noticed a girl who seems, a particularly energetic and horrible example of the Party norms. She does more of the Party work than is necessary; she looks over-puritanical; she shouts more than others during the two minutes Hate programmes; and in every other way she shows her zeal for the Party. Winston finds that this girl is frequently looking at him. He thinks her to be an agent of the Thought Police. Then one day, she slips a piece of paper into his hand. The words on this piece of paper are: "*I Love You*" (96). The rest of the book is largely concerned with the resultant loveaffair between Winston and Julia. Here is a private passion which defies Party rules, a passion strong enough to make a man and a woman act independently. No wonder, the Party thinks it necessary to crush this passion.

Julia turns out to be by no means an ardent revolutionary, not an intellectual. She just wants some uninhibited sex, mingled with tender feeling. Somehow she has preserved her power of natural joy against the conditioning of the Party. She has secretly had sexual intercourse with a number of other Outer Party members already. She now wants Winston as her lover. But it is exactly this assertion of the natural human desire which constitutes a revolt against the Party. Winston and Julia begin with great difficulty to create a secret private life for themselves. The preservation of Julia's sexual normality has led her to regard the whole Party ideology as rubbish, though this sexual normality does not prompt Julia to any kind of action. In an intellectual like Winston it is sure to lead to thoughts of revolt.

The novel is splendidly executed up to this point. But from the moment at which Winston and Julia are arrested and their interrogation and torture begin, the book deteriorates. It is not that Orwell's powers of imagination has failed. The fact is that the subject of physical torture is one with which Orwell is not equipped to deal. The result is that Orwell's pre-occupation with torture and terror gives his book a note of the strangled cry. In other words, the book now acquires an agonized and frenzied note. What gives it its frenzy is probably that it is the work of a dying man, because when Orwell has written it he has been already at an advanced stage of tuberculosis.

Nineteen Eighty Four can be a love-story. It is so, however, on two levels showing two kinds of love, the false and the true, human and the divine. The first is exposed before the second is accepted, though it is by the agency of the partial and inadequate love that the erring soul is brought to the fullness of truth. Winston's human or earthly love is centered upon Julia, the girl who also works in the Ministry of Truth and like him, turns out to be a rebel against it. The objection may very justly be made that Winston's love for Julia has very little of the genuinely earthly about it. From the beginning, with its reversal of the usual accepted roles, Julia's being all the initiative, Winston remaining passive all the way, it is an unconvincing affair at least as an affair of flesh and blood. It has no other manifestation. Even they admit as much when it appears that they make love not so much from mutual desire but as an act of rebellion against the rule they hate.

Orwell at some point does not want to idealise Julia, dwelling on her 'practical' turn of mind, her ruthlessness and impatience with theory. It is difficult to believe in except as a fantasy of sexual relations, cut off from responsibility and even from any deeply-felt sexuality. Winston's sadistic day-dreams about her before he gets to know her and when he thinks of her hatefully as "young and pretty and sexless"(13), are nearer to the mark, perhaps more than Orwell has intended. She is in fact a kind of intersex, her "swift, athletic movements" (8), and "boyishness" being particularly noted. The "atmosphere of hockey fields and cold baths and community hikes"(8), that Winston first perceives about her, the badge of the Junior Anti-Sex League that she wears, are more appropriate than they are meant to be but they are intended to be no more than a disguise beneath which her passions are hidden.

In the beginning, Winston suspects Julia of being an agent of the Thought police. Perhaps that is exactly what she is. She may be regarded as an agent whose function is to trap an individual's consciousness and lead it where it would not go. Her's is a shallow and false love, which nevertheless prepares Winston for the true love that he seeks. She is, no more than part of the process which starts with the keeping of his illicit diary and leads inevitably to the torture-cellars of the Ministry of Love. But she is the instrument, by which he is brought out of his total isolation and comparative safety into the danger of feeling. She appears from nowhere, she has no history; and in her rather dubious femininity she is not much more for Winston than an extension of himself. But, even to think of her as a day-dream, she does represent the possibility of something happening in Winston's soul. She is the means by which the experience of suffering can be extended, even if it is still essentially Winston's own suffering.

A critic, Isaac Deutsher, in his article "1984-The Mysticism of Cruelty" in *Russia and Transition and Other Essays*, explains the behaviour of Oceania's rulers. According to this critic, then, Orwell does not entirely accept any of the usual socio-economic theories about the aims of totalitarianism. It happens, however, that neither this critic nor anyone else has yet been able to provide a satisfactory explanation for that systematic excess in destroying human values which is a central trait of totalitarianism. Orwell is, therefore, justified in acknowledging his helplessness before the ultimate meaning of totalitarianism. Nor can one deny that Orwell has given in this novel the most graphic vision of totalitarianism that has yet been composed. If the world as described in *Nineteen Eighty-Four* does actually exist one day, no one will read this novel, except may be the rulers who will be surprised by its prophetic power. If such a world does not actually take a shape, people will feel that this book has been merely an expression of its author's private disturbance, a description of a nightmare which the author has seen in his sick bed.

The main reason why Orwell has switched to fantasy seems to have been his feeling that the documentary and realistic novel has failed to have the desired impact on the readers. Possibly the appeal to reason in such novels has failed to convey a sense of urgency. He also seems to have felt that the new developments in the political sphere in his time cannot be explained adequately in the documentary and realistic mode. The world has become deeply irrational since Orwell's young manhood and he feels that the glaring insanity of his generation can be adequately dealt with, only by venturing beyond the boundaries of reason. The new developments of his time might be summed up as totalitarianism, genocide, the resurgence of dictatorship and fanatical nationalism and the revival of political imprisonment and torture. Obviously, a form is needed which will give him sufficient freedom to invent a form which would rely on the power of the imagination rather than the accuracy of observation. That is the reason for his writing of his two fantasies *Animal Farm* and *Nineteen Eighty-Four*.

In these two books, Orwell makes use of the fear that man's worst nightmares might one day prove to be true. To deal with such elemental subject-matter, realistic fiction is simply inadequate. Only an anti-utopia can displace a utopian vision. Only the fear of hell can be as powerful as the desire for heaven. In *Nineteen Eighty-Four*, Orwell has tried to make his readers sensitive to what it will mean to live in a totalitarian State. In such a society a constant vigilance and control are exercised over the citizens. Naturally, Orwell has intended his novel for readers, who have hardly any direct experience of totalitarianism. If the purpose of Orwell's book is to make people to resist totalitarianism by exposing its nature and methods, the utter defeat of his hero is hardly apt to strengthen their resolve. If the meagre powers of a clerk like Winston Smith help to rise successfully against the mighty O'Brien and Oceania, then the danger that they present would not appear so real or prophetic. No doubt that this book has produced a certain degree of effect upon the readers. The fact that much of the vocabulary of the book has passed into common use shows that Orwell has been successful in achieving his purpose.

Nineteen Eighty-Four can be approached either as a novel, embodying a political argument or as an indictment of materialism, cast in fictional form. As a novel, it is straightforward. The hero, Winston Smith is a civil servant, verging upon middle age who is unable to adjust himself to the totalitarian system under which he works. He falls in love with a clerk in his office, is arrested for holding subversive views and, after much physical and mental suffering repudiates both his opinions and his girl. Winston Smith himself is portrayed with convincing detail; the girl, Julia, is not intended to be much more than a lay figure; and the remaining characters loom as gigantic thunder clouds of terror or drift past the narrative in trails of mist. The Inferno atmosphere of the story is cunningly created and well maintained. Orwell's purpose, however, is not to compose a romance with an unhappy ending. He sets out to write a cautionary tale, by which to convince the terrible results which will follow it. Ignorance will allow the humanistic heritage to be submerged in a flood of materialism.

The nightmare of Orwell's future is that there is no future. O'Brien defines this future as a boot, stamped for ever upon a human face. This future is the prison of the perpetuated present in which the only things which change. They are technological advances combined with the actions of political groups, worshipping their own power, making the present ever more inescapable, a present in which there is no human freedom. It is a future governed by power, war, propaganda, brain-washing, espionage, and police terror, all continuously "improved" by machinery. The novelist has been criticised for being too pessimistic in *Nineteen Eighty-Four.* It is said that the novel offers hardly any hope for the future criticism but it is, however, unjust. Orwell's novel sets out reasonably to demonstrate despair, for it is about the possibility processes of a totally politicised world being State; it is about the possibility of love and joy becoming utterly impossible.

The conditions described in this novel are likely to take shape one day or not. If Orwell's vision expresses a real possibility, then one should not expect the consolations of love or hope or joy in the book. He brings out the fear into the consciousness of the people. He, in fact, issues the warning that all independent personal values will be replaced by social conditioning. Orwell is not concerned so much with the rocket-bombs, telecasters, and other mechanical inventions as with ideologies, systems of thinking, methods of persuasion, and propaganda. They enslave men's thinking to such an extent that the only hope for the future will be in the lives of those who do not think but merely work and play, namely the proles. Orwell's starting-point is, therefore, "a study of the machine, a genie that man has thoughtlessly let out of its bottle and cannot put back again".(2)

Thus, in *Nineteen Eighty-Four,* Orwell is concerned with the fear that man may use machinery in order to condition his own consciousness. He may make himself a machine at the service of a centralised controlling ideology. In the concluding scene O'Brien convinces Winston that freedom is slavery, and two plus two make five and then he forces him to love Big Brother. It is the electric shock administered to him, by O'Brien operating a machine, which causes Winston to submit. The victimisation of Winston means the atomisation of the individual consciousness by the Party leaders whose minds and lives have become completely identified with theory. The actions are dictated by an abstract necessity. The operation of political philosophy upon individual human beings is impossible without machinery. Orwell in his novel imagines, a world in which authority would become a reactor smashing human atoms. He also imagines that the world will be split into three super world States fighting one another perpetually. Orwell assumes that the seeds, of the future lay in the politics of the time at which he has been writing. He foresees in effect the extension of symptoms produced during World War II. He is of the opinion that the western and the eastern allies, would turn against one another, and that each unit would become a huge police State with concentration camps, rationing of goods and people always under control.

One can very well understand that *Nineteen Eighty –Four* is a dystopian novel for varied salient features of the dystopian novel are well presented in it. The main aspect is that these types of novels portray the destiny of an individual in a society which is well advanced technologically. The protagonist Winston Smith suffers physically, mentally and morally in a terribly upsetting community. Every right of him is curtailed and every minute activity of him is not only watched but also monitored. The protagonist who is a human of flesh and blood becomes devoid of any sort of feeling and emotion in course of time, for such is the treatment that he gets from a fully equipped, well advanced society. Science with its gigantic steps is so quick and fast on its path of progress, but ironically has done nothing constructive for the individual. It has only led Winston Smith towards destruction and doom. Everything is so obnoxious in the deplorable totalitarian society and Orwell has presented the fate of his protagonist in such a way, with all the skill of his craftsmanship as a writer, so that it reaches the brain of the reader with a bang so as to create ripples of awareness in the sea of thought.

A CLOCKWORK ORANGE

Anthony Burgess is a powerful and energetic novelist. He is accepted as one of the cleverest and most original writers of his generation. This versatile novelist has achieved a worldwide reputation as one of the leading novelists of his day. Malcolm Bradbury in *Independent On Sunday*, pays a glorious tribute to Burgees as “the great post modern store house of British writing... an independent experimentalist”. This British novelist is considered to be one of the newest and most talented of the younger British writers. Many critics have rated his novel *A Clockwork Orange* as one of Burgess' most brilliant achievements. Hyman, an American critic and educator in his review, in *The New Leader* acknowledges Burgess as a satirist and calls the novel as an eloquent and shocking one that is quite unique.

The ability of an individual to make moral choices is the major theme of *A Clockwork Orange.* The society presented by Burgess deals with experiments and behaviour modification techniques on criminals. The citizens should be given the choice of choosing between the good and the evil. The state should not interfere and destroy the capacity of an individual making his choice between the good and evil. Burgess points out that destroying the ability to choose evil also destroys the capacity to choose good. In the name of justice and security, the state also commits violence just like the protagonist Alex and his gang members. Julian Mitchell an English novelist, playwright and critic in his article, "Horrorshow on Amis Adventure" in *The Spectator,* points out that,

> Mixing horror with farce in his inimitable manner, Mr. Burgess develops his theme brilliantly, though there is a certain arbitrariness about the plot which is slightly irritating and I find it difficult to accept the concentration that being young is like being a clockwork toy-you walk into things all time. (662)

A special edition of *A Clockwork Orange* by Andrew Biswell, sheds light on the enduring fascination of the book's sweet and juicy criminality and the red streak of gleeful evil running through it. Anthony Burgess in his "Clockwork Marmalade" in *The Listener* discusses the violence and reacts to criticism. He reveals that,

> … *A Clockwork Orange* was intended to be a sort of tract, even a sermon, on the importance of the power of choice. My hero or anti-hero, Alex, is very vicious, perhaps even impossibly so, his viciousness is not the product of genetic or social conditioning: it is his own thing, embarked on in full awareness. Alex is evil, not merely misguided, and in a properly run society such evil as he enacts must be checked and punished. (197)

The London youngster's culture has covered groups, referred to as teddy boys, mods, and rockers. The teddy boys have made the appearance in the nineteen fifties, as England has been economically improving from World War II. Like many youth subcultures, they have turned out to shock the reputation quo, wearing Edwardian-style drape jackets, suede Gibson footwear with thick crepe soles, slender trousers, and loud ties like the greasers in the films inclusive of 'American Graffiti'. The teddy boys have listened to 'rock and roll', and have clashed with rival gangs regularly with 'razors' and 'knives' and have been engaged in random destruction. With the British pop music increasing in the 1960s, many teddy boys have become rockers, wearing leather jackets, hanging out in working class pubs, and using motorcycles. Burgess discusses the violence in *A Clockwork Orange*,in his "Clockwork Marmalade" in *The Listener* as thus,

> …The youth of the last fifties were restless and naughty, dissatisfied with the post conspicuous than mere old time crooks and hoods were what many people meant when they talked about growing criminality. Looking back from a peak of violence, we can see the British deady boys and mods and rockers were mere tyros in the graft of anti social aggression: nevertheless, they were a portent, and the man in the street was right to be sacred. (197)

The 'mods', a brief term for modernists, have additionally emerged during the late nineteen sixties in England, an elite group other than the teddy boys. They cut their hair short, ride scooters, wear military heavy weather proof jackets and introduce new dance movements. The mods have been called 'rude boys,' and developed into the 'punks' and 'skinheads' of the 1970s. According to Burgess, being a mod, a stilyaqi, or a teddyboy, means someone who has practiced character freedom. They do whatever they want to right from the way of dressing. In fact they express their freedom through their mode of dressing. These participants of the new style of freedom, in a way also help in the new consumerism. Their life style has indeed helped the growth of economy. But the so called freedom of dressing up, in a way looks like an attitude of slavery when they exhibit a sort of fascination and addiction for the new method of haircut and dressing. Burgess hates the control of the country over the individual. He believes that character freedom will be curtailed. This country control has been nowhere greater evident than inside the Soviet Union in the early nineteen sixties. Burgess has noticed the extent to which the communist government has regulated the individual's life. He especially hates the manner wherein communism has shifted the ethical responsibility from the individual to the kingdom.

Britain has become a democratic government, in the nineteen fifties. The Labour party's celebration has nationalised many industries which include coal (1946), power (1947), and the railways also (1948). In 1946, the National Health Service has been found to take care of the British residents medical needs. This welfare state has become terrible to Burgess. He believes that, it has positioned the desires of society as supreme over the liberty of the character. Narrated in the first person, the novel portrays the ultraviolent life of Alex. He is a teenage hoodlumsin a future English society which is governed by hypocritical and self service officials; moreover, the society is terrorised by street gangs. Robert K. Morris is an American critic and educator and a biographer. In "The Bitter Fruits of Freedom," in *The Consolations of Ambiguity: An Essay on the Novels of Anthony Burgess* he describes, "Alex, gross product of welfare state over kill, is not depraved because he is deprived but because he is indulged. "Myself," he notes rather pathetically at the beginning of *A Clockwork Orange*, I couldn't help a bit of disappointment at things as they were those days. Nothing to fight against really.

Everything as easy as kiss my sharies". (55) Alex is violent but a lover of music, a born leader but is disowned by his droogs. Robert K. Morris further reveals that,

> Alex's Utopia is more than the result of suprapermissiveness and self gratification; it is the consequence of the "original sin" inborn with every offspring of modern organisational leviathans. Having discovered that existence has always meant freedom, but never having been taught "goodness," Alex responds predictably and inevitably to the killing burden of choice. (57)

A Clockwork Orange opens with Alex, the fundamental character of the novel. His droogs, Faint, Pete, and Georgie, are drinking drug-bound milk at the Korova Milkbar. After leaving the Milkbar, the four confer what is to be done. They indulge in ultraviolent acts which include the inhuman beating of an old man assigning library books and also happen to destroy his books. Next, the group runs over an opponent group in a distribution centre. Billyboy, the pioneer, and his five droogs are assaulting a youthful devotchka (young lady). Alex's team assaults them, beating them back until the millicents (police) arrive. Alex and his group next go to a house with HOME on the front door. This marks a turn in the novel towards the fabular (fantastical), and far from the realistic. After telling the lady that his companion is sick and he needs to use her telephone, Alex breaks into the house with his group, now wearing covers.

Alex and his gang beat the lady's husband violently, spoil the house and then they assault the lady. The man, F. Alexander, is an author writing a book called *A Clockwork*

Orange, which Alex calls as a gloopy title. The book attacks the welfare state as an abuse on common freedom by the government. The droogs demolish the book. This scene echoes an incident from 1943 in Burgess' own life, when his spouse has been assaulted and brutalised by a group of American warriors. Anthony Burgess has an interesting and tragic history before he has written this novel. Again in the 1940's, the American GI's (American army) have robbed and beat Burges's wife. This also has contributed to the scene in the book where F. Alexander's spouse has been raped and crushed by Alex and his gang.

Later in the 1960's, Burgess spends some time in Russia. Hence, he has tried to substitute the nadast language, instead of English. At first, the book has been written without the nadast, but Burgess has gone through it to rewrite it. Nadast is the language invented by Burgess, especially for Alex and his cronies and droogs. It is comprised of distorted English and Russian words. Robert O Evans, an American critic and educator in his article, "Nadast: The Argot and Its Implications in Anthony Burgess' *A Clockwork Orange", in Journal of Modern Literature,* describe the company of Alex and his three friends:

> They are called droogs, the Russian word for friend slightly Anglicized. They are making up their rasso docks (Russian minds) what to do that evening. The times are skorry (sorry). There is no law yet against some of the new vesches (things) they put into moloko(milk) to give one a horrorshoe(good) feeling. Their pocketsare full of deng (money). They decide to tolchock (push, pound) and old veck (man) in an alley. The

> viddy (see) him swim in his own blood. They consider doing violence to some starry(old) ptitsas (birds, feminine; women). They go away smecking (languhing) with the contents of a till. (406)

Anthony Burgess has written his first draft of *A Clockwork Orange*, when he and his wife have taken a journey to Leningrad now St. Petersburg, then the Soviet Union in 1961. According to Andrew Biswell in the "Introduction" of his special edition of the novel, "Burgess and his wife saw gangs of youths who were violent and well-dressed, not unlike the Teddy Boys back in England" (xiii). Biswell then continues to point out that these gangs made Burgess realise that "dandified, lawless youth is an international phenomenon, equally visible on both sides of the Iron Curtain (xiii).

Burgess is horrified and captivated during that journey,to see the roaming gangs of gangsters, known as Stilyaqi. Burgess has seen how the police, worried over the ideological crimes against the nation, have a difficult time in controlling these unruly violent youths. He moreover, has noted down the similarities of the Russian and British cultures of the teenagers. The British country has turned to fashion a criminal character with complex ways. These children speak, act, and try to be Russian and English. As a result, Alex and his droogs also involve themselves in activities of violence. Droog is a word derived from the Russian word 'drugi', which means buddies in violence. The stilyaqi, or style-boys are the ones, who have emerged in Russia at some stage in the 1940s.They are more or less contemporary with the American 'beats'. The stilyaqi have listened to 'jazz' and later to American 'rock and roll'. The Soviet government has taken this into consideration and is worried about the juveniles. After coming back to the

Milkbar, Alex hits Dim for criticising a lady, singing musical drama at the bar.Georgie and Pete side with Dim and Pete mentions that,

> If the truth is known, Alex, you shouldn't have given old Dim that uncalled-for tolchock. I'll say it once and no more. I say it with all respect, but if it had been me you'd given it to you'd have to answer. I say no more." And he drowned his litso in his milk-glass. I could feel myself getting all razdraz inside, but I tried to cover it, saying calm: 'There has to be a leader. Discipline there has to be Right?' None of them skazatted a word or nodded even. I got more razdraz inside, calmer out. (34)

Alex comes back to his home and falls asleep while listening to Beethoven's music. In the morning, his Post Corrective Advisor, P. R. Deltoid, visits him. He warns him that one day the police will get him if he proceeds with his troubles. After Deltoid's departure, Alex visits a music store, where he picks up two young ladies. He takes them back to his flat, gives them alcohol drinks, and assaults them. At the Milkbar, Pete, Georgie, and Dim persuade and convince Alex that they have to ransack a bigger house. Alex makes the arrangement, to show that he is a decent brother and pioneer. That night, they break into the place of an elderly rich lady who is feeding her cats. She battles with Alex, and he knocks her out with one of her statues. At that point Alex tries to escape on hearing the police sirens. Dim hits him with his chain, thumping him out. The police men arrive and capture Alex, as Georgie, Pete, and Dim abandon him. They take him to a cell, where Deltoid, spits in his face. Alex later learns that the old lady he has battled with has died of heart attack. Alex says, "That was everything. I thought of all those kots and koshkas mewling for moloko and getting none, not any more from their starry forella of a mistress. That was everything. I'd done the lot, now. And me still only fifteen" (81).

The second part of the novel that, sections eight through fourteen, portrays Alex's life in the "staja" (State prison), after he is sentenced to fourteen years there. Alex makes quick friends with the priest, who permits him to listen to classical music on the house of prayer stereo. The jail authorities and the minister of the Interior acknowledge that if the droogs want to be recognised with their generation, a generation that is generally violent, the droogs too need to be violent. Youth violence, however, is nothing new. It has existed for centuries. It is possible that Alex's violence stems from the fact that he is just a youth. Simply growing up may be a cause for violence. Arendt Hannah a Jewish, American, political theorist in her book *On Violence* remarks on behaviour like this:

> Their behavior has been blamed on all kinds of social and psychological factors on too much permissiveness in their upbringing in America and on an explosive reaction to too much authority in Germany and Japan, on the lack of freedom in Eastern Europe and too much freedom in the West, on the disastrous lack of jobs for sociology students in France and the superabundance of careers in nearly all fields in the United States all of which appear locally plausible enough but are clearly contradicted by the fact that the student rebellion is a global phenomenon. (15)

Alex has the chance to experience Ludovico's Technique, a trial treatment. It ensures his discharge from jail and guarantees that he will never return, and Alex approves. Burgess models the possibility of Ludovico's Technique on the work of B. F. Skinner who is, a mid-twentieth-century behavioural psychologist. According to him, the general public whether it be of young or old, should be either rewarded or punished according to their good and bad activities. This will not only motivate them to do good keeping in view the reward but will also induce a fear in them to keep away from unpleasant activities thinking of the punishment. He trusts that human conduct can be moulded. The individuals are willing to adjust once they figure out how to partner "good" conduct with the joy of the reward they get for it. He partners "bad" conduct with the pain of punishment. These techniques are utilised for a period on juvenile delinquents and slow down kids. Skinner the behaviorist defines his thoughts in his book *Beyond Freedom and Dignity*. For two weeks, Alex is given injections of a medication that makes him physically sick whenever he witnesses rough acts. With his eyelids open, Alex is compelled to watch movies pressed with scenes of torture, rape, and beating. The film scenes of Nazi barbarities from World War II, with Beethoven's Fifth Symphony as its sound track, make Alex to hate violence and Beethoven, whose music he loves.

The rules and norms are thus redrawn for Alex. The old ones are reinforced and a new one is added. Music is accidentally involved, for Beethoven has used it as a background music in one of the films. Previously a source of joy, the music that meant so much to Alex, has now become associated with pain,

> I don't mind about the ultra-violence … I put up with that. But it's not fair on the music. … Then Dr Brodsky said: "Delimitation is always difficult. The world is one, life is one. The sweetest and most heavenly of activities

> partake in some measure of violence – the act of love, for instance; music for instance. You must take your chance, boy. The choice has been all yours. (91-2)

After the treatment, Alex is paraded before a board of jail and state authorities. At that time he cowers before a tormentor, who is challenging him to fight. Alex himself is shocked by his own abusive reaction to a lovely lady. Now, he has been exposed of free will to pick his actions. Dr. Brodsky declares him fit for release from the jail.

In the third segment of the novel, Alex turns into a victim. In his absence, Alex's parents have taken a guest, Joe. Alex is compelled go to the lanes. He is forced to be with the general population whom he has victimised as seen in the first part. He is being beaten by a gathering of old men in the Public Biblio (library), one of whom Alex and his group have beaten earlier. Alex is then rescued by three policemen, two of whom end up being Billyboy and Dim. The government has enrolled the two in its activities to utilise society's criminal workings for its own evil purposes. Billyboy and Dim take Alex out, beat him and abandon him for dead. Alex then wanders through a town and happens to see the house with "HOME" written on the door. F. Alexander, the author who has been beaten by Alex before, identifies Alex from the daily paper. He takes him in, wanting to utilise him in a campaign. He shares his thoughts with Alex saying,

> I think that you can help dislodge this overbearing Government. To turn a decent young man into a piece of clockwork should not, surely, be seen as any triumph for any government, save one that boasts of its repressiveness. He was still wiping this same plate. I said..... (31)

Alexander and his liberal companions make plans to utilise Alex as an example of government repression. The author recognises Alex as the person who has beaten him up and has raped his wife a couple of years back. With the help of his friends, Alexander keeps Alex in a flat and plays classical music namely, Otto Skadelig's Symphony Number Three and thus drives Alex to think of suicide. As a result of the sickness and pain he does not want to listen to the music. Alex jumps out of the window, yet does not die. He is admitted in the hospital, with his love for brutality being re established. In the mean time, the Minister of the Interior visits Alex. He offers Alex a well paid job in exchange for his support of the government. In the last part, Alex is back at the Korova Milkbar, this time with another gathering of droogs, who take after the old gathering. In spite of the fact that they take part in ultraviolent acts, Alex gives orders and watches. He is "old" now, eighteen. He meets one of his previous group members, Pete, who is married and works for an insurance agency. Alex starts to day dream about being married and having kids:

> Youth must go, ah yes. But youth is only being in a way like it might be an animal. No, it is not just like being an animal so much as being one of these malenky toys you viddy being sold in the streets, like little chellovecks made out of tin and with a spring inside and then a winding handle on the outside and you wind it up grrrgrrrgrrr and off it itties, like walking, O my brothers. (211)

A Clockwork Orange explores the ideas of evil by asking what it matters to be a human. Alex chooses evil due to the fact that it is right in his nature to achieve this. His impulse in the direction of desirable is produced because it comes from out of doors. It is instilled by a government bent on controlling the population by controlling their goals. By using the Ludovico technique on Alex, the government gets rid of the issue that constitutes his humanity, and his freedom to pick. They deal with the symptom, of Alex's evil, oblivious of its own complicity in his behaviour. For Burgess, an evil Alex is a human Alex, the most popular. He has been programmed to deny his very own nature.

F. Alexander, the author whom Alex and his droogs beat up, is one of the mouthpieces for this concept. At one point he tells Alex, "They have turned you into something other than a human being. You have no power of choice any longer. You are committed to socially acceptable acts, a little machine capable only of good" (177). Later, he adds, "the essential intention [of the Ludovico Technique] is the real sin. A man who cannot choose ceases to be a man."(174).The repetition of Alex's word "what's it going to be then, eh?"(147), underscores the topic of loose will and the preference of being a woman or a man. *A Clockwork Orange* pits against the intrusive powers of the nation in opposition to the liberties of the person. Burgess looks at the connection among the country and the man or woman in a society that has deteriorated and is on the brink of anarchy. Left to its personal gadgets, the country will try to manipulate the individual via regulation, and brutality.

This is evident in the way wherein Alex is used by the country as an example of its strength to "rehabilitate" criminals. Instead of rehabilitating them, they reprogram them and brainwash them. The cynical energy-mongering of the state is embodied in the character of the Minister of the Interior. He manipulates Alex, first into volunteering for the Ludovico method, after which into siding with the government. After Alex's suicidal attempt, he strives and returns to his evil nature. Burgess indicates that personal liberties which include freedom of speech and expression are beaten in such a society. The novelist implies that individuals must both understand and take delivery of their evil nature. They should recognise how society attempts to stifle it. Alex does not seem to understand the implications of the Ludovico technique. When it is explained to him, he is not aware of his own nature and how society has helped to shape it. He sounds philosophical, expressing the importance of self: The authorities and the judges and the colleges cannot permit the bad because they permit the self. Alex knows that he is evil, and tells readers, "What I do I do because I like to do" (45). The novel implies that his insight is greater than most of the people's insight. He accepts himself for who he is, instead of hiding at the back of others and the authorities. He reveals no guilt for his moves. However he embraces evil and revels in his evil side.

Burgess' moral in *A Clockwork Orange*, may be defined as a struggle among Augustinianism and Pelagianism. Augustinianism is derived from St. Augustine (354-430), who believes in humankind's innate depravity. Pelagianism is derived from Pelagius (c. 355-c. 425), whose doctrine holds that people have been perfect and that evil becomes the end result of superstition, social forces, the surroundings, and so on. In

Burgess' novel, the government clings to Pelagius like thinking that it tries to trade humans, to turn them far from their evil behaviour via something essential. In Alex's case, it is the Ludovico method. Alex, who embraces his evil nature as if it is a second pore and skin chooses to be, that way. However he suggests the promise of selecting a special way within the book's very last bankruptcy. Burgess is not the consummate Augustinian that some critics have made him out to be. The tug of war between Augustinianism and Pelagianism creates the ethical tension that sustains Alex's story. But it is a tension that stays in large part unresolved.

A totalitarian government interferes with the individual's way of life and breaks them into a condition of obedience. Anthony Burgess' novel, *A Clockwork Orange*, is a nightmarish vision of future Britain. The behavioural adjustment is taken to unsafe extremes in the protective measure for saving the request of a disconnected society. The novel is self-depicted as a general public in its tragic hours, in the beginnings of totalitarianism where Alex, a fifteen year-old criminal views the world through an adolescent lens. Through these two ideal models, Burgess demonstrates the gathering of people that denotes a society as "dystopian" in the absence of a good decision. The novelist uses this to reveal the crude motivation of a dystopia, the ordering of social control and proficiency over human nature.

The dystopian novel *A Clockwork Orange* is told through the individual portrayal of Alex, together with his band of droogs; he takes the night life into his own hands, cruelly carrying out the wrongdoings of homicide, assault, and burglary. In one of their most appalling violations, Alex and his friends force their way into the home of a couple, where they assault the lady, as her significant other is compelled to watch. The turning activity comes when Alex discovers that his companions are double crossers, setting him up one night to be gotten by the police. After sometime in an over-swarmed jail, Alex is advised that there is an approach to be discharged back into society. He has to undergo the Ludovico technique, an imaginative and primitive type of treatment that cures culprits.

In *A Clockwork Orange,* technology is used to benefit the State and government. By turning the criminals into law-abiding citizens with Ludovico's Technique, the State is seemingly doing something good. However, Alex's personal space, body and brain are invaded and transgressed by the State, or the "big machines," that is supposed to protect its citizens. The individual's rights are violated for the good of the majority. Alex loses his freedom of choice. This becomes evident when Dr. Branom talks with Alex, after his first Ludovico session. He tells him,

> Violence is a very horrible thing. That's what you're learning now. Your body is learning it." … "Life is a very wonderful thing," said DrBranom in a like very holy goloss. "The processes of life, the make-up of the human organism, who can fully understand these miracles? … What is happening to you now is what should happen to any normal healthy human organism contemplating the actions of the forces of evil … You are being made sane, you are being made healthy. (121)

Good behaviour and the norms of society are thus imposed upon Alex. He decides what is to be considered as 'sane', 'healthy' or 'normal' It seems that it is most beneficial for the state to recommend itself to the people who are not too independent in their thoughts. Thus the state condemns people like Alex, who are not likely to rebel to undergo Ludovico's Technique. The supposed goodness and crime reducing ways of the State raise more suspicion. Alex questions the authenticity of one of the violent films he is made to watch, this time portraying a gang rape situation. Echoing from the novel,

> This was real, very real, though if you thought about it properly you couldn't imagine lewdies actually agreeing to having all this done to them in a film, and if these films were made by the Good or the State you couldn't imagine them being allowed to take these films without like interfering with what was going on. So it must have been very clever what they call cutting or editing or some such veshch. For it was very real. … I began to feel sick. (116)

Alex volunteers to be the guinea pig for this examination, just to find out the reality about the strategy. He is pumped with sickening medication and strapped down to a seat with his eyelids open, and is compelled to watch awful scenes of brutality in films. He is under the misery of sickening medications and without the capacity to move his body; he is traditionally adapted to partner scenes of brutality and sentiments of agony with overpowering physical ailment. A teen must find out who he or she is, and find out what kind of values that are important. But last but not least, he or she must find out to who he or she wishes to belong to. The teenagers must find their place in society, and that can be a very frustrating and stressful time. That time may also result in an identity crisis. To explain identity crisis, Larsen & Buss in their book, *Personality Psychology. Domains of Knowledge about Human Nature* point out,

> Erikson (1968) coined the phrase identity crisis, meaning the feelings of anxiety that accompany efforts to define or redefine one's own individuality and social reputation. For most people, the process of going through an identity crisis is an important and memorable phase of life. Sometimes it happens early, in adolescence; sometimes it happens later, in midlife. (444-445)

Alex, the primary hero of the novel is frustrated with the life he lives and he despises the standards which he declines to take after. He feels that there is no future he can seek after: "I couldn't help a bit of disappointment at things as they were those days. Nothing to fight against really. Everything as easy as kiss-my-sharries. Still, the night was still very young". (15). Then again, he is mindful that the well being of such vacancy is the legislature of the leader of the State. Alex reprimands the lack of response of the general public, which is the consequence of a large scale of control by the power. Along these lines, he endeavours to avoid himself from this ruinous impact. Alex communicates his obliviousness and state of mind towards the administration by his savage conduct. He attests his unrestrained choice through building up a pack of droogs and beating men, burglarising or assaulting ladies. The fundamental hero has no expectation to apologise or assume any liability for his horrible demonstrations. Alex communicates his indifference thus, "We hadn't done much, I know, but that was only like the start of the evening and I make no appy polly loggies to thee or thine for that. The knives in the milk - plus were stabbing away nice and horrorshow now" (10).

This profane strike will later result in response of the administration to confine Alex's further disturbance of the State's framework despite the fact that Alex knows about the risks and discipline which could fail if he is not demoralised from his rough conduct. On the contrary, Alex looks for more provocative occasions since he realises that it causes the harm to the dependability of the administration. In addition, it fortifies his push to oppose his oppressors and he feels the need of making some move against the State. The hero is captured after he assaults an old lady who is on her way and kicks the bucket. Alex is arrested by the police. He communicates his assessment of the power. He is portrayed as a delegate of a deceitful descent that he would not like to be related with. He describes how ,"The millicents now got down to making this long statement for me to sign, and I thought to myself, Hell and blast you all, if all you bastards are on the side of the Good then I'm glad I belong to the other shop. "All right," I said to them," (77).

By communicating such individual contemplations, the principle hero starts his rebellion and battles with the framework. It is obvious that Alex has the mettle to resource his choice and that the administration does not speak of any risk for him. After the capture, Alex is controlled in jail and he is obliged to acknowledge certain rules. For example, the expressions of the song which is sung amid the administrations in the Wing House of prayer. It expresses 'a great intention' of the state to change Alex and the detainees into kind and loyal men: "Weak tea are we, new brewed But stirring make all strong. We eat no angel's food, Our times of trial are long" (90). The State's definition of an immaculate human relates to its endorsed controls. At this stage, the administration starts to apply the limitations to Alex since he has to be 'treated' of his 'illness'. All things considered, the hero does not understand the risk or the outcome which he may endure later on.

Alex is picked up as the primary contender for an examination with the Ludovicos Technique. The reasons of this choice are three angles trademark for Alex. He is youthful, strong and horrible. The legislature does not have to make Alex to experience this procedure as he trusts it at the start of his flexibility. He intentionally picks this 'fast' route for his discharge from jail. In reality he loses his free will. He is not aware of effects of this Reclamation Treatment that has on his identity and uniqueness. Then again, the point of the Priest of the Interior is clear. He tells them, "You can use him as a trailblazer. He's young, bold, and vicious. Brodsky will deal with him tomorrow and you can sit in and watch Brodsky. It works all right, don't worry about that. This vicious young hoodlum will be transformed out of all recognition"(103).

There are negative parts of the Ludovico's Technique. The Jail Chaplain wants to know whether the Technique can make a man decent and he questions its consequences for the casualties. He himself has grave doubts about it. Quoting from the text, "I must confess I share those doubts. The question is whether such a technique can really make a man good. Goodness comes from within, 6655321. Goodness is something chosen. When a man cannot choose he ceases to be a man". (93). The clergyman additionally demonstrates that being great is not a triumph in all circumstances. It is a certain notice and an endeavour to demoralise Alex from being required simultaneously,

> It may not be nice to be good, little 6655321. It may be horrible to be good. And when I say that to you I realize how self-contradictory that sounds. I know I shall have many sleepless nights about this. What does God want? Does God want goodness or the choice of goodness? Is a man who chooses the bad perhaps in some way better than a man who has the good imposed upon him. (106)

In any case, Alex chooses his own destiny by understanding and by marking a structure for the test. In The New State Institute for Reclamation of Criminal Types, the spot of Alex's treatment, the hero describes how he, " was led off to a very nice white clean bedroom with curtains and a bedside lamp, and just the one bed in it", (108). In the first place, Alex does not consider this spot as a jail. The surroundings just delude his faculties and hide the way that he cannot escape from there. His opportunity is confined by the bolted entryway and bars on the window. This environment increases Alex's tension, which is the main sign that the hero feels about the weight and encroachment of his freedom. Doctor Brodsky tries to convince Alex that there is no reason for denying the treatment and that it is helpful for him. "Don't fight against it, please. There's no point in your fighting. You can't get the better of us." (129). Brodsky demands giving a decision to Alex: "You must take your chance, boy. The choice has been all yours." (130). The hero gets misdirected by a benevolent tone and by the guarantee of the advantages he may get on account of participation with the legislature. However, it is clear that Alex believes that this promise will lead to his submission later.

Alex tries to deceive Doctor Brodsky during the treatment, and imagines his dismissal of savage conduct. Brodsky finds out this double dealing and depicts a condition in which Alex can accomplish full recovery. He conveys his thoughts in these words: "You're not cured yet. There's still a lot to be done. Only when your body reacts promptly and violently to violence, as to a snake, without further help from us, without medication, only then - "(130).This announcement characterises the last results of the control with Alex's identity. It will never again a characteristic response of the hero. Specialist Brodsky, the fundamental coordinator of Alex's change, at last achieves his objective. Alex takes after the named standards and considers a fitting path as per Brodsky. By the procedure of the rehabilitation Alex is decreased to a clockwork orange, the term utilised as the title of the book, composed by F. Alexander. He clarifies the expression as, "the attempt to impose upon man, a creature of growth and capable of sweetness, to ooze juicily at the last round the bearded lips of God, to attempt to impose, I say, laws and conditions appropriate to a mechanical creation, against this I raise my sword-pen" (25).

The creator of this announcement makes it clear how the free individual is able to do self improvement changes, like a modified machine. The feedback of the legislature and of the manipulative methods are shown for taking control of the enemy. During the last phase of the treatment, Alex is seen by the gathering of people to witness the accomplishment of the test. Dr. Brodsky reports the outcome, to the gathering of people, "Our subject is, you see, impelled towards the good by, paradoxically, being impelled toward evil. The intention to act violently is accompanied by strong feeling of physical distress. To counter these subjects has to switch to a diametrically opposed attitude". (140).

This declaration portrays the coldblooded and damaging effects of Alex's previous brutal conduct. The administration tries to convince the crowd that the State wishes for the prosperity of the general public. It additionally cautions how one may end in the event if he tries to restrict the administration. At the end of the day, the Prison Chaplain opposes the after effects of the treatment. He contends that Alex has been denied of his essential right, right to have a decision. To quote him,

> "Choice," rumbled a rich deep goloss. I viddied it belonged to the prison charlie. "He has no real choice, has he? Self-interest, fear of physical pain, drove him to that grotesque act of selfabasement. Its insincerity was clearly to be seen. He ceases to be a wrongdoer. He ceases also to be a creature capable of moral choice". (140-141)

Then again, an educator who is likewise a member of the control indicates that Alex has no privilege to whine: "You have no cause to grumble, boy. You made your choice and all this is a consequence of your choice. Whatever now ensues is what you yourself have chosen." (141). Despite the fact that Alex cannot settle on his own choices any more, he makes his last attempt at the change of the circumstances, "Me, me, me.

How about me? Where do I come into all this? Am I just some animal or dog?" And that started them off govoreeting real loud and throwing slovos at me. So I creeched louder, still creeching: "Am I just to be like a clockwork orange?" (141).

Alex communicates his grievances of the control with his choice. He understands what has been done to his uniqueness. This exertion demonstrates the last resistance to the power. However it does not demonstrate any effective result or accomplishment. On the contrary, the legislature lays the fault on Alex and induces him that his good wantonness is the result of his own choice. At last, Doctor Brodsky gloating on his productive achievement of the Ludovico's Technique, portrays Alex's potential future to the gathering of people, thus,

> He will be your true Christian," Dr. Brodsky was creeching out, "ready to turn the other cheek, ready to be crucified rather than crucify, sick to the very heart at the thought even of killing a fly." And that was right, brothers, because when he said that I thought of killing a fly and felt just that tiny bit sick, but I pushed the sickness and pain back by thinking of the fly being fed with bits of sugar and looked after like a bleeding pet and all that cal.'Reclamation,' he creeched. Joy before the Angels of God. (143)

After Alex is sent out from the Institute, he understands that no one thinks about him in the outside world. He encounters detachment and isolation: "Nobody wants or loves me. I've suffered and suffered and suffered and everybody wants me to go on suffering" (154). In this manner, Alex considers going back to jail as opposed to being a part of the misleading society that disdains him. This dismissal, speaks of the lethal impact of the administrative investigations and the purpose behind the good decay of the hero. Alex's isolation brings out considerations of death which he finds as the main salvation: "The empty glass on the table and wanting to cry and feeling like death was the only answer to everything" (159). Alex's sadness, step by step increases until the minute when it gets to be intolerable. He thinks about the main plausibility which can safeguard him from his misery a suicide attempt. His last thoughts are a source of solace and trust in his urgent condition: "Open the window to fresh air, fresh ideas, a new way of living." And so I knew that was like telling me to finish it all off" (188). After the attempt to take his own life, Alex exposes notoriety of the government. It is considered as a disappointment of the system in which the power lays its trusts on. The news in the daily papers mirror the circumstances like this,

> Out of one glazz I could read like headlines which were sort of trembling in the rooker of the chelloveck that held them, like BOY VICTIM OF CRIMINAL REFORM SCHEME and GOVERNMENT AS MURDERER and there was like a picture of a veck that looked familiar to me and it said OUT OUTOUT, and that would be the Minister of the Inferior or Interior". (192)

This report means the failure of the power and a specific trust in the hero. The administration is compelled to concede its issue and to expel the damage which has been done to Alex due to the Ludovico's Technique. In this way, Alex will get the compensation for his past endurance. The changes that Alex undergoes before and after the Ludovico Technique is based on the context of the three part structural model of psyche conceived by psychoanalysist Freud. He refers it as id, ego and super ego. In his *New Introductory Lectures on Psychoanalysis,* he relates the id to basic human drives and impulses, describing it as "a striving to bring about the satisfaction of the instinctual needs subject to the observance of the pleasure principle" (105-106). While the id acts on the 'pleasure principle,' the ego focuses on the 'reality principle' by attempting to merge the basic passions of the id with the constraints of reality. The super-ego namely the psychic agency disapproves the id. Super ego forces punishment, for socially unacceptable behaviour, with feelings of guilt or remorse.

There is a general lack of interest in the youth generation. The movies are heavily controlled by the government. There are few spare time offers for the youths in *A Clockwork Orange* because the government values work and not joyful laziness. A clear example of this is when Alex describes the municipal painting in his flat block where the people's faces are 'stern in the dignity of labour' (35). In addition, as Alex contemplates, "the government does not go into the goodness of things" (31). There is a lack of interest, a lack of recreational offers, a glorification of work and restriction of free will. According to Charles A. Nelson, a psychologist and Floyd E. Bloom, a medical researcher, the co authors of the book *Brain, Mind and Behavior* explain the results of boredom and of drug abuse. To quote them,

> Human beings seem to have two compelling but contradictory needs: we like things to stay the same (to be familiar) and we crave novelty. We

> search for substances that will get us out of our rut drug abusers often report that they take drugs to relieve boredom and substances that calm our anxiety when things become too unpredictable. (318)

A neglect and a restriction of free will create boredom. It makes people take drugs, which again increases violence. In many ways the government in *A Clockwork Orange* has thus created the violence problem in the younger generation. Drugs, together with the government's neglect, may be the cause for youth violence in *A Clockwork Orange*. There are more elements in the novel that cause violence. The drug abuse is not the only reason. After this occurrence Alex discovers that he has been reestablished to his own self. He appreciates having considerations of unlawful conduct at the end of the day. It is the after effect of intercession of the government. It has chosen to return Alex's personality through a "deep hypnopaedia". According to the clergyman, Alex by all accounts has been cured at this stage. He is given another chance and it is just his decision how he will choose his further activities and future. In spite of the fact that Alex puts stock in his recovered opportunity, he unconsciously abides to the necessities of the government. He agrees with a backing and cooperation with the State. The pastor is satisified of his triumph and imagines friendship with Alex. He informs Alex that,

> I and the Government of which I am a member want you to regard us as friends. Yes, friends. We have put you right, yes? You are getting the best of treatment. We never wished you harm, but there are some who did and do. And I think you know who those are. (198)

The power is obliged to forsake the past goal to control Alex. It is important to guarantee Alex's participation with the State. This coordinated effort speaks to the persisting impact of the legislature on Alex and his unrestrained choice. Then again, Alex holds back his human kindness and communicates his ethical decision when he chooses to act criminally again. He dreams of brutality while he listens to the Beethoven's Ninth Symphony,

> When it came to the Scherzo I could viddy myself very clear running and running on like very light and mysterious nogas, carving the whole litso of the creeching world with my cut-throat britva. And there was the slow movement and the lovely last singing movement still to come. I was cured all right. (199)

When Alex is released into the society, Burgess pushes this thought forward. The impacts of the Ludovico system have basically rendered Alex as an android. Although he wishes to have the experience of undergoing 'feelings' his body just does not cooperate for it and it only exhibits lack of involvement and survival impulses. Just looking through a therapeutic book in a library is sufficient enough to stimulate sickness in him. What Burgess appears to emphasis here is that when unrestrained choice is taken from one, feeling is wiped out also. To be alive is to see both endurance and joy through experience, craftsmanship, and connections with the world. It implies having the desire to encounter each feeling on the human range. One can just see the magnificence when they are interested in the full human experience that lies behind the great and terrible impossibility.

Alex tries to listen to Mozart, a craftsman, whom he identifies with himself. Listening to it sickens him since he relates it with the uproarious sounds of the music utilised as a part of the vicious recordings he has watched. It is a key point in the novel when the group of onlookers understand some qualities. The qualities that are associated with independence, innovativeness, craftsmanship, identity are being taken away from him. The unrestrained choice and an oppressed world wipe out the humaneness and freedom of human beings. F. Alexander recommends to Alex in the novel as thus:

> "Rest, rest, poor lad," he said, turning the tap on so that all steam came burping out. "You've sinned, I suppose, but your punishment has been out of all proportion. They have turned you into something other than a human being. You have no power of choice any longer. You are committed to socially acceptable acts, a little machine capable only of good. And I see that clearly – that business about the marginal conditionings. Music and the sexual act, literature and art, all must be a source now not of pleasure but of pain". (174)

Alex is no more physically a perfect timing orange but rationally a perfect timing orange in the brain produced in a difficult totalitarian culture. Alex's brutality stems significantly from his dissatisfaction, associated with his need to have a place in the public eye, even a totalitarian one. That is something involving savagery on a general level. Savagery, then, comes accordingly between a fragile relationship between human's characteristic need to have a place and the structure of society. Savagery is not simply science. It is only a side effect of society, yet a collaboration between the two things, having a place and dissatisfaction. That seems to be the principle impulsion to brutality. There is a contention amongst mankind and the control of a state. For a state to be totally proficient, human delicacy must be expelled from the framework. One cannot exist without the other. One cannot be a human without the capacity to pick amongst great and abhorred people. In Burgess' words, the alteration of the most enthusiastic people into machines, namely the perfect timing oranges paves the way for a tragic country.

A Clockwork Orange uses the thought of dystopian society to inspect the intricacies of human instinct. For Burgess, human instinct has the capacity to settle on individual choices about ethical quality. Basically, an oppressed world is an administration that picks what is simple over what is right. It organises the control of the state over the opportunity of the person. The contention is introduced to the group of onlookers through the portrayal of a totalitarian culture in its exceptionally primal structure. Afterwards, it indicates how it follows up on the youthful and enthusiastic characters of the story. Burgess' vision is an amazing one, since he does not just recount dystopian elements. He utilises the idea to uncover all inclusive and critical part of being human. He does not become mixed up in the semantics behind the different tragic attributes. Rather, he uncovers what utopian and dystopian worlds can let one know about their own inclination. In this way, *A Clockwork Orange* is greatly pervasive for this time, not just as an intriguing work in the dystopian sub kind.

The extremely terrible thoughts symbolise remaining flexibility and independence in the protagonist's identity. The perusers may say that Alex's change is something to be thankful for. He has changed, and he has grown up, by that working in the National Gramodisc Archives. For him, safeguarding music is a great deal more useful than thrashing individuals into a bloody mess. Alex has sold away his freedom and his mankind. Now he is a precision orange, working for the totalitarian machine. A machine that confines through and through freedom. It also keeps independence at a sheltered separation.

Then again, to make bargains when entering adulthood is something just about everybody does. Individuals surrender some of their flexibility when they take up mortgages and commit themselves to work and paying charges for a long time. Making a trade-off amongst independence and having a place within society is how the world works. Alex is truly the same as a great many people. He too needs a position of his own, a spouse and kid, and to accomplish that, he should surrender some of his standards. It is some portion of growing up. What makes Alex accommodating and so discouraging, is that he offers to a totalitarian development, not a fair one. Also, that is the reason the novel's end is a bit discouraging on the grounds, that the administration deletes such an extensive amount of embodiment of human.

At the end, the totalitarian development has won. That is the genuine risk a totalitarian development speaks of. The development's savagery, risk of holding individuals down, is the genuine threat. Essentially in the light of the fact that, it is so hard to battle. Mozart, Beethoven, Disraeli are special people and vital figures in the public arena whom Alex identifies himself with. Alex surrenders at the end of the novel. Comparing himself, with Mozart, he says that he has not refined anything. His work in National Grammodisc Archives is not an achievement. Alex has no different fields in which he can fulfill anything in a totalitarian culture, similar to the society in *A Clockwork Orange*. There is no spot for independence, or decision. Alex's sort of viciousness is the main thing that has transformed from the first section of the book till the last. The savage Alex is a part of what has changed from physical, singular savagery, to methodical, political, prohibitive, harsh, totalitarian brutality.

A Clockwork Orange has evoked controversy since it has been first published. The violent content of the novel is criticised by the critics. There have been many debates focused on the function and interpretation of Burges's ending. Robert K.Morris the American critic, educator and biographer, in his article "The Bitter Fruits of Freedom" in *The Consolations of Ambiguity* describes Burgess like this: "Like all good satirists, Burgess lashes out, with savage indignation at stupidity and blind error and lacerates our disastrous pretensions at solving human problem at the expense of human beings."(55). Concluding on notes of 'joy', Burgess firmly believes that the individual is endowed with regenerative powers. Without doubt the novels message is acknowledged as radical and moderate as the style through which it is expressed. In *Critical Essays on Anthony Burgess*, edited by Geoffrey Aggeler, he states, "Both as satire and linguistic tour de force, A Clockwork Orange is one of Burgess' most brilliant achievements" (121).

One cannot miss streak of hideous surrealism running, through the novels of Burgess. In *Clockwork Orange* a nightmarish fantasy of future England has become thoroughly infernal. Anthony Burgess the novelist, is frank enough to reveal his own opinion in his own novel *A Clockwork Orange* thus,

> I'm not particularly of *A Clockwork Orange*, because it has all the faults which I rail against in fiction. it's didactic. One may excuse any author for writing what he writes, because he's primarily earning a living, you see. He's turning out an artifact which will, he hopes, sell enough to pay the rent. It's Balzacian. It's almost, indeed, it's Shakespearean. Nothing wrong with it. But I do object very strongly to this thesis that is written on the damn book. The book is not all that interesting or important. (448)

The society's brutality is more threatening to Burgess than the person's power which is human, extensive, and undertrained. Burgess, commenting on *A Clockwork Orange*, has indicated that he meant to encourage a contrast between Alex's brutality and society's. Burgess explains that the violence in the novel is simply extra to show what state can do. William H. Pritchard, an American critic and educator in his, "The Novels of Anthony Burgess," in *The Massachusetts Review*, feels that Burgess has succeeded in bringing out the defense of self and condemnation of state. He compliments Burgess thus, “Within its odd but carefully observed limits, the book is entirely consistent, successful and even pleasing, Burgess most eye and ear catching performance" (539). Not only Alex is the victim of the author; the readers also come of age, in reading the novel and is excited about the advancement and growth.

A dystopian novel has various characteristic features of which the threat of punishment and death is one of the dominant one. The protagonist of the novel *A Clockwise Orange* Alex belongs to the 'most modern' group and the very outlook of his life is totally different; culture and heritage has no role to play at all. They are completely eradicated from their lives and they live in a well advanced technical world, where one can hear echoes of totalitarianism. Here in this novel, Burgess has vividly presented the role of the government which seems to be antisocial and antihuman. 'Antisocial' in the sense that the government is not considerate towards the society. In the name of 'welfare', they are very dominating and try to execute their own ideas not thinking whether it would be beneficial or good to the society. The sole idea behind the government is nothing shorter than absolute power. The individual is compelled to follow the rules and regulations of the government and are threatened with severe painful action even if there is a slightest display of disobedience or rather refusal from the side of the individual. Thus Alex, is controlled totally by the government and this totalitarian society presented in the novel makes it a perfect dystopian one.

THE CHILDREN OF MEN

P.D. James is a popular British writer and her novels are noted for their well constructed plots, strong characterisation, psychological realism and descriptive prose. She rose to fame for her series of detective novels, starring police commander and poet Adam Dalgliesh. She differs from the other typical writers of thrillers. Her characters with complex motives and particular features are portrayed meticulously. She excels in filling her settings with wonderous details. Her *The Children of Men,* a dystopian fiction is about technology, human reproduction and the rights of women. This novel praised for its excellent characterisation, is scary and full of suspense. Many book reviews point out that the novel is taut terrifying and ultimately convincing. She herself wonders about, the confusing mixture of good and evil; faith and failure; love and a dangerous self sufficiency. Soo Darcy, in her essay, "Power, Surveillance and Reproductive Technology in P. D. James' *The Children of Men*" places, the novel "within a subgenre of dystopian fiction about technology, human reproduction, and the rights of women"(1).

This observant and one of the rare writers is known for her descriptive passages and her plots. She firmly believes in the choices, made by the people. This novel with scary images and a brooding sense of evils has all the potential to become a classic. Once again recalling the words of Soo Darcy, from her article,

> James' novel, then, can be situated within a body of work that represents a renewal of interest in dystopian themes in the late 1980s and early 1990s, particularly that, which engages with contemporary concerns about

> reproduction, engaging with shifting cultural attitudes towards the emerging reproductive technologies and modes of control and surveillance of the pregnant body. James herself is quoted as saying that the novel "was [inspired by] the review of a scientific book drawing attention to a dramatic drop in the sperm count of Western men" (1995), clearly demonstrating the close link between women's writing and cultural concerns about fertility and reproduction. (4)

The setting for *The Children of Men*, a dystopian novel is a world of mass infertility. Dr. Theodore Faron, the protagonist is a doctor of philosophy and a historian of the Victorian age at Oxford University. He is divorced, a solitary man and a self confessed failure: "I don't want anyone to look to me, he confesses. He adds further, not for love, not for anything" (26). P.D. James vents her anger against the decline and fall of the modern world, using Dr. Theo as her mouth piece. Zan Lyppiatt, is the Warden of England, an equivalent position of the prime minister. His regime initially appears to be good. He provides comfort for the ageing population, which results in voter's apathy "'I am not a tyrant, but I can't afford to be merciful. Whatever it is necessary to do, I shall do.' He looked at Theo, who thought for one extraordinary moment that he saw in Xan's eyes, a plea for understanding" (121).

The novel is narrated in both first person and third person, and begins in the year 1995, known as the Year Omega. The fall in the population is due to various reasons, such as birth control, abortion and the spread of AIDS. Nanelle R. Brash and David R. Brash in, "Biology, Culture, and Persistent Literary Dystopia" point out that,

> dystopian science fiction share the theme of, "denial of biology" a denial of human's basic needs. The prospect of genetic continuity is completely absent a prospect that "is the motivation underlying sex, love, and indeed everything in the organic world". Infertility, not only means the absence of children, but, worse, the absence of hope and sense of purpose. When we lose purpose, we simply give up since there is nothing to fight and struggle for. When Theo sees his cousin Nigel's fancy home, he blankly asks, "years from now there won't be one sad to look at any of this. What keeps going?" Nigel then comfortably replies, "I just don't think about it." This short conversation adequately sums up the apathy and ignorance that the sense of hopelessness dangerously ingrains into people's mindset. (228)

Depression is unavoidable as the human species is dying out. As men are infertile it is a doomed civilization under the control of Xan, the dictator. A solution is sought out by all the countries under the United Nations. As the years are gone, individual research efforts are taken to find a cure and solution. The children born in 1995 are known as the Omega. When these children reach sexual maturity, the human extension has become a reality. The Omegas are men to produce fertile sperm, as the suicide rate has escalated. Xan imposes a fine in order to stop the epidemic. From Theo's entries in his diary, it is revealed how suicide is encouraged among the dependent and incapacitated elderly people. Xan attempts to put an end to depression and illness by releasing various funds.

A group of dissidents who believe that Xan is a dictator are ready to launch their revolution. They want Theo to present their demands to his cousin. They call themselves as the Five Fishes.

> The mass emigrations, the great internal tumults, the religious and tribal wars of the 1990s have given way to a universal anomie which leaves crops unsown and unharvested, animals neglected, starvation, civil war, the grabbing from the weak by the strong. We see reversions to old myths, old superstitions, even to human sacrifice, sometimes on a massive scale. That the country has been largely spared this universal catastrophe is due to the five people round this table. (98)

Xan firmly refuses to their demands of shutting down the penal colony, putting an end to the orgainised suicide of the elderly dependents and holding an election. Xan is the president of a country that has become a prison. Britain has come of age. It is an amiable prison, a veritably Dostoevskyan dystopia.

The Five Fishes have decided to carry on their revolution. Distributing political pamphlets and destroying the wharves is their first step. Theo is meeting with his cousin Xan, with full Council of England and it is not a successful one. The Council members are angry with him. Theo has turned down the offer of Xan to be his advisor. Xan warns Theo, of the forthcoming action against the dissidents. The visit from the Secret police unnerves Theo. Moreover he is confused about his feelings for Julian. She is described as “dark-haired, a honey-coloured woman, long necked with high cheekbones, wide-set eyes whose colour [Theo] couldn’t determine under strong straight brows, a long narrow nose, slightly humped, and a wide, beautifully shaped mouth. It was a pre-Raphaelite face. Rossetti would have liked to paint her" (39).

Theo travels around Europe for many months. On his return, he learns that the revolution is still going on. Motivated by his feelings for Julian, he agrees to help the Five Fishes. Theo comes to know of Julian's pregnancy and joins the dissidents who try to run away from the State of Security Police. This group consists of Rolf, the husband of Julian, Luke the priest, and Miriam the midwife. The mutual hatred between Theo and Rolf, changes Rolf into a betrayer. Luke is bashed to death by the Omega. It is revealed later that Luke is the father of the unborn baby. The Omegas are spoilt, notorious for their ego, youthful, luxurious life style, violent, remote and unstable. To find a safe place for the birth of the baby, Theo, Julian and Miriam leave for a wood land near Oxford.

The birth of baby boy marks the beginning of a new era. Miriam is garroted, probably by Xan when she goes to fetch water. Theo and Xan shoot at each other in their final face off. While Xan misses his aim, Theo hits his cousin in the heart. The Coronation Ring is removed from Xan's finger and is placed on Theo's finger. The Ring is a symbol of authority. Theo seems to be poised to become the new leader of the United Kingdom. Theo introduces the baby boy as the symbol of fertility and hope, to Council. He has succeeded in finding both love and power. Quoting from the novel, "Theo christens the baby in his own name and that of its dead biological father. It sees him assume a trio of rights over the baby: paternal, religious and political"(243).

P.D. James' novel is scary, suspenseful, fascinating and as well as frightening. With a potential to become a classic, this novel displays a constant struggle for power. She is successful in the unraveling of humankind with her keen observation. Monarchy is gone. But Xan, Theo's cousin, the self appointed Warden of Britain fulfill the role of a monarch. He has the absolute power in his control. He does not hold elections because he is so sure of winning. All ideas of the improvement of the society, justice, reform, love and hope depend on the existence of the future generation. James Bowman in "Our Childless Dystopia" says that, " It was reasonable to struggle, to suffer, perhaps even to die, for a more just, a more compassionate society, writes P.D. James, but not in a world with no future where, all too soon, the very words 'justice,' 'compassion,' 'society,' 'struggle', 'evil', would be unheard echoes on empty air" (108).

Initially Xan's rule seems to be benign, going out to provide the best in difficult circumstances. The role of Warden of England represents the ultimate power in the novel. Xan himself does not enjoy it, as he struggles with the power. He cannot think of retirement even though he no longer relishes it. Many people covet for that position but Xan is conceited enough to think that no one is fit for the role. XanLyppiatt's rule has transformed almost insignificantly. Rolf notes that, "the Warden was elected when he first took power, but that was fifteen years ago. He hasn't called an election since. He claims to rule by the people's will, but what he is a despot and a tyrant" (57). The theme of fertility and reproduction, is connected with the political power, which seeks control over two things namely, the medico-scientific institution and the population of England. Soo Darcy says that,

> Under Xan's regime, the body is disciplined through a series of systems and controls that echo Foucault's description of a drive towards both increased usefulness—through, it is hoped, the discovery of a fertile human—and docility that allows the population to be ruled without disorder. (8)

Julian is afraid of becoming the focus of the dormant technology, and the power. Such practices are shown to constitute system of surveillance and management of pregnant women and their behaviour.

The Five Fishes, the tiny dissident group who are against Xan, undertake a struggle for power. Their goal is to become the voice of the voiceless population. For different reasons they want power individually. Miriam wants to avenge the death of her brother. In order to decide the place of her baby's birth, Julian wants the freedom that comes along with power. The greedy betrayer who is not actually the father of the baby seeks the ultimate power. He believes that he deserves it because of being the father of a child in a barren species. He is disappointed and frustrated to know that Luke is father of the child. This is the turning point in the novel. He realises that his only power is an insider's knowledge and turns into a betrayer. Moreover, Theo gets an absolute power over the Five Fishes and becomes their protector. After witnessing the intense labouring of birth, with wonder and awe, Theo wishes to become the father of the child.

Theo has never before coveted the power of the Warden of England. But he is forced to assume this powerful position. He accepts the position of the guardian of the child readily and, also donning the Coronation ring, the wedding ring of England as "a gesture to assert authority and ensure protection" (240). Theo himself is becoming intoxicated by the power of the ring. He admits that "it begins again, with jealousy, with treachery, with violence, with murder, with this ring on my finger" (240). Symbolically the ring provides him of the spousal rights over Julian. Being the Warden he does not need to marry Julian in order to have control over her. He has good intention and sympathetic feelings towards Julian. The critic Walter Wangerin in *The New York Time Book Review*, points out that,

> … as Faron grows to love Julian, love is purged of personal return. In the time of endings, choices are reduced to the most basic, for self or for others, and those who choose selflessness choose genuine sacrifice, dying for Julian who believes she is pregnant and for the sake of the future.(245)

Reproduction is highlighted as the central theme of *The Children of Men.* P.D. James in her novel represents a renewal of interest in dystopian themes in the late 1980s and early 1990s. She brings out the contemporary concerns such as reproduction, shifting cultural attitudes, reproductive technologies and mode of control, and surveillance of pregnant baby. The bleak concept of the novel is based on two possible outcomes. The human race faces extinction. The last generation to be born will have a lonely future. The second possibility is that the last fertility can be restored to some extent. P.D. James successfully connects a childless future and a waning not waxing (increasing) of political passions. Theo's aged, former tutor, Jasper expresses his sentiments about the impending end of humankind, thus,

> On the whole, I'm glad; you can't mourn for unborn grandchildren when there never was a hope of them. This planet is doomed any way… If man is doomed to perish, then universal infertility in as painless a way as any. And there are, after all, personal compensation. For the last sixty years we have sycophantically pandered to most ignorant, the most criminal and the most selfish section of society. (44-45)

The presence and absence of love is one of the themes, handled by P.D. James. The Warden of England shares a common bond of inability to love his cousin Theo. Theo declares, "I couldn't then say what for nearly forty years I have known to be true. I don't want anyone to look to me, not for protection, not for happiness, not for love, not for anything" (26).

Theo has never loved his wife and has never loved his daughter either. Julian, one of the Five Fishes is a passionate and religious person. Theo is drawn towards her. He can see beauty in something as simple as a tree. When she asks for help to fight against his cousin Xan, the Warden of England, he is ready to do it. Even when he finds out the truth that Luke the priest is the father of the child, he is ready to protect her. Theo has been distanced from other people throughout this novel. Gradually he falls in love with Julian even though he still has a long way to go in his journey towards emotional enlightment. His poetic description of his own feeling when he spots Julian in the market throws more light on his emotional love for her,

> I was seized with a ludicrous urge to dash to the flower-stall, press notes into the florist'shands, seize from their tubs the bundles of daffodils,

> tulips, hot-house roses and lilies, pile them into her arms and take the bag from her encumbered shoulder. It was a romantic impulse, childish and ridiculous, which I hadn't felt since I was a boy. I had distrusted and resented it then. Now it appalled me by its strength, its irrationality, its destructive potential. (131)

The end of the novel describes the birth of Julian's baby boy. His birth symbolises the beginning of a new era. Infertility is maintained as the masculine problem. Theo the new Warden of England plans to marry Julian and present the baby to the world as his own. His emotional awakening has started. He has seen the beauty of a birth leading to a new beginning. Quoting from the novel,

> Theo thought: It begins again, with jealousy, with treachery, with violence, with murder, with this ring on my finger. He looked down at the great sapphire in its glitter of diamonds, at the ruby cross, twisting the ring, aware of its weight. Placing it on his hand had been instinctive and yet deliberate, a gesture to assert authority and ensure protection. (240)

Theo's tears fall over that forehead of the child. He recollects the rite from his childhood memory. He makes the signs of cross on the forehead of the child, with his thumb, wet with his own tears and stained with her blood. Love is the ultimate prize in Theo's journey. P.D. James depicts a world, where there has been no birth for over twenty years. The novelist alternates between the third person and first person in the form of a diary that has been kept by Theo, an Oxford don. GenaCorea in *The Mother Machine*(1985) has discussed that,

> Despite the fact that Theo is not the biological father of the child, his behaviour can be examined using the model of ownership. Corea compares a woman's physical experience of maternity, through the changes to her body and the resultant labour and birth, with an "abstract idea" of paternity that results from the nine month gap between the moment of conception and the birth of the baby that a man must claim as his own. Corea asserts that "[m]an's sperm is alienated (that is, separated) from him in the sex act and this alienation negates him as a parent". (287)

Although the novel opens in the year 2021, the origin of events, start in 1994, Year of Omega. The sperm count of human males has gone down to zero. Imminent extinction is faced by mankind. Omegas are the last people to be born "A race apart". Various prerogatives are enjoyed by the Omegas. Human beings lead a meaningless life. The elderly people become a burden to others and the society. So they go quietly to the Quietus, a mass suicide site. This primitive notion is to prevent misery and not, putting them out of their misery. Heavily sedated elderly people are taken to face 'willing suicides'. That is the idea told by the government. But Theo sees it as a real murder. The old life is devalued. But the youngest generation Omegas are the opposite. They hold a God like status. Omegas, members of the generation born in 1995 are given a series of social privileges. They love to display their given social superiority, physically:

> The female Omegas have a different beauty, classical, remote, listless, without animation or energy. They have their distinctive style which other women never copy, perhaps fear to copy. They wear their hair long and loose, their foreheads bound with braid or ribbon, plain or plaited. It is a style which suits only the classically beautiful face, with its high forehead and large, widely spaced eyes. Like their male counterparts, they seem incapable of human sympathy. (10)

The Omegas are described as spoilt, over entitled, egoistical, violent, remote, and proud of their youth and luxurious life style. They do not even try to disguise their contempt for the non Omega elders. The citizens are compelled to learn skills for survival. After luring the foreign workers, they exploit them. Omegas, from poor countries called as foreign Omegas or 'Sojourners' are forced to carry out undesirable work. At sixty, they are discarded like rubbish and sent back. Fearing the loss of labourers, emigration is denied to Omegas.

The fate of the Sojourners is better, when compared to the plight of prisoners. The Sojourners are denied of British citizenship and are deported when they outlive their function. The prophecy concerning the elderly is the most troubling aspect. The senile or infirm are subjected to a state sponsored program called 'the Quietus'. When the elderly are unable to "make a contribution to society," they are drugged and sent out to sea for drowning. Ralph C. Wood a Professor of Religion at Wake Forest University, in his work "Rapidly Rises the Morning Tide", an essay on P.D. James's *The Children of Men* says that,

> The cruelty of their embarkation is disguised with a spurious festivity. A band plays such grotesquely ironic tunes as "Bye, Bye, Blackbird," "Somewhere over the Rainbow," and "Abide with Me." The women wear white robes and clutch posies as if they were brides, some of them lifting their skirts as they sing and sway in addled piroutess. One doddering lady, perhaps having been medicated too lightly, refuses to go gently into the night of her "good death". (285)

After twenty five years of the birth of the last human, people find themselves in a helpless and hopeless situation. A lingering hope of discovering a cure fades. Leading a devalued life, people are naturally depressed. In this utter hopeless atmosphere, they even lose interest in the simple pleasures of sex. Theo is rejected and depressed as he also lives a life without hope. Feeling defeated and unworthy his only goal in life is to die at Wool combe. Jasper Palme Smith, a friend and teacher of Theo commits suicide, due to lack of hope. His sick wife dies in the Quietus. Jasper is on the run with the Five Fishes. Julian is given a God like status, when she becomes pregnant. Her surprising pregnancy shoots a burst of hope, for both Theo and human kind. It is hailed as a miracle birth since human species is saved from extinction. Julian hopes about the birth of other children. It will help her to lead a normal life. The fearsome members of the Council pay their humble respect to the first of a new generation.

The women Rankein and Harriet Marwood take one step further and go near the baby boy. Carl Inglebach says, 'so it begins again'. Theo exclaims, "This birth is the concern of the whole world, not just England. The child belongs to mankind," to which Luke responds, "The child belongs to God" (179).Thus Julian's pregnant body and the baby it contains, are bound up in discourses of ownership that draw upon a web of power relations incorporating the conflicting facets of government, religion and the autonomy of the individual . In biological sense, Theo is detached. In the very words of the novelist,

> Theo thought: It begins again, with jealousy, with treachery, with violence, with murder, with this ring on my finger. He looked down at the great sapphire in its glitter of diamonds, at the ruby cross, twisting the ring, aware of its weight. Placing it on his hand had been instinctive and yet deliberate, a gesture to assert authority and ensure protection. He had known that the Grenadiers would come armed. (240)

Theo makes use of social structure to claim the baby as his own. The structure of the novel is comprised of two books. The Book one called as Omega, refers to the infertility of the human race and the last generation moving closer to death. Alpha refers to the ultimate winner of the Alpha male. It can be taken as a reference to Theo's victory over Xan, or the birth of the baby. Theo succeeds in protecting Julian and the baby from the government. His win over his tyrant cousin assumes the fact that the "baby is born free". The structure of the novel with its two parts 'Omega' and 'Alpha' reflects the sense of endings and beginnings. David Curry in his article, "Nativity and Resurrection in P.D.James' *The Children of Men*" says that,

> The first describes the wasteland where the pleasures of the present in a dying world are, like T.S. Eliot's "fragments" of the 12 past, "no more than pathetic and crumbling defenses shored up against our ruins". The past, too, is empty of vitality and meaning for the present. It is barren of purpose. (11)

Alpha signals the possibilities of new a beginning. The novelist is sure that the past is redeemed through repentance, recollection and the growing awareness of the necessities of love. Theo is aware of the gulf between him and Julian's belief. He may be unable to connect with the God of her faith. But he accepts the possibility that, in the end the bridge would be love. A reason to love comes from the barren wasteland. He recollects and his eyes are filled with tears, promising everlasting life. He is assured of redemption. To quote P.D. James from the novel,

> There was very little water left in the bottle, but he hardly needed it. His tears were falling now over the child's forehead. From some far childhood memory he recalled the rite. The water had to flow, there were words which had to be said. It was with a thumb wet with his own tears and stained with her blood that he made on the child's forehead the sign of the cross. (241)

Water and blood; nativity and resurrection gain significance. The human beings have to learn the lessons of love. A kind of mystical power is embedded in blood feels McCarthy in "The Symbolism of Blood and Sacrifice". He says that, "it is a divine sanguinary substance which revivifies the divinity and so gives force to rites".(166) The loss of blood means death and weakness. *The Children of Men* can be considered as a religious allegory. It is highly disturbing for the author and the reader to narrate the christening in blood. The new born baby is branded with cross, since he has arrived after so much depression, death and misery. He is a link between life and death. After so many years of infertility he is born. So he is elevated. But in future he will be subjected to unwanted samples and experiments. According to the prominent literary figure and feminist, Adrienne Rich in "Of Woman Born: Motherhood as Experience and Institution," "the mother faces a range of painful, socially weighted choices: abortion, suicide, abandonment of the child, infanticide [..] whatever her choice, her body has undergone irreversible changes, her mind will never be the same, her future as a woman has been shaped by the event of pregnancy and birth" (12).

There are two types of pre-existing oppression on the experience of motherhood. One is that the important relationship of any woman towards her children and her power to respond to them. The second one is the aim of institution that all women should remain under the control of men. Men have attributed to women a divine quality, a form of worship of a goddess. Perhaps they are afraid of being controlled and overwhelmed by women. The feminist, Adrienne Rich in *Of Women Born: Motherhood as Experience and Institution*, says that maternity has been shaped by male domination. For her, "the experience of motherhood as we know it is constructed and loaded with the burden of how mothers are supposed to feel and act based on males' arbitrary opinions" (14).

The New York Book Review compliments the novelist for her subtle characterisation, "Her view is Olympian… Always she explores character, the complexities of motive, and thought and emotion; and always she wonders about the nature of humankind in general, this baffling mixture of good and evil, faith and failure, love and a murderous self sufficiency" (15). She is known for her insightful and sharply etched characterisation. She is gifted with her keen observation power that helps her to make her characters memorable. Her narrative is also compelling. Theo, the hero is the narrator and also the main character of the novel. His diary throws light and an insight, on his character. His unhappiness is revealed exposing his inner thoughts and actions. Theo happens to overhear the conversation of his grandparents. It is actually the comparison between Theo and his cousin Xan, now the Warden of England. The conversation goes like this, "I sometimes wonder if Theo won't go further than Xan in the end. Oh no. Theo is a good-looking, intelligent boy, but Xan is brilliant"(18).

Xan becomes the Warden of England later and demands unquestioning and undemanding and unemotional obedience. He is able to make the population to accept his policies. They believe that his polices are in the best interest of the people. When the Five Fishes contact him, this thought begins to change. Five Fishes the small group of rebels approach Theo, asking him to intercede with Xan on their behalf. They are Ralph, Julian, Miriam, Gascoinage, and Luke. The political pamphlets are distributed by them. They perform guerilla attacks. To quote from the summary in *Masterpiece and World Literature,*

> Rolf, the putative father, revels in his singularity, not wanting the Warden to "take over," proclaiming the birth to the world on television and "showing my child to the nation"; that, he announces, is "for me to do, not him." To Theo's comment that the "birth is the concern of the whole world" and the baby "belongs to mankind," Luke replies, "The child belongs to God". (1)

P.D James portrays all her characters, with a masterly stroke like an artist with a brush. Theo is questioning the purpose of resistance and rebellion in a world without future. P.D. James picturises the Omega, the last generation of human as aloof and dispassionate. Other than the Five Fishes and Omegas, the rest of the population live, in a numb stupor. The academician Alan Jacobs in his book, *Life's Value* says that, "of all James' novels, *The Children of Men* is probably the most pointed in its social criticism, certainly the deepest in its theological reflection" (48). P.D. James has been placed among the great social novelists of nineteenth century England, especially George Eliot, the eminent Victorian with the masculine pen name. P.D. James offers a moral critique of the society. Through her novel she tries to answer the waxing troublesome questions in a radically new way. She gives a warning that the human race is going to witness a dreadful and wonderful union of human evil and divine grace.

Christianity is the key to P.D. James' fictions. As a novelist she seeks to make her faith to be understood rather than comparable. James is an artist and her moral instruction is given in an indirect manner. She is not a prophet to seek conversion by directly declaring the divine Word. Her novel focuses on enormous subtlety of evil even though the central characters are people to be despised. She wants people to understand and even pity them. She describes both pagans and Christians alike, what people least wish to hear. Her novel is a futuristic fantasy- part thriller, part allegory and part cautionary tale. It is set in the Britain of the year 2021. A mysterious global disease has cost the entire human race to lose its fertility. This novel can be described as a Christian dystopian. Not only she warns but also foretells that wrath and destruction are already upon the people. The only way out is the way of divine deliverance. People long for a new life which becomes an universal obsession. Ralph C. Wood, in his, "Rapidly Rises the Morning Tide" says that,

> Macabre things happen in this craven new world without children. Kittens are christened in their place. New dolls are dressed up and wheeled about in prams; broken ones are buried ceremoniously in consecrated ground. Woman experience false pregnancies and pseudo births. With a mania at once sinister and sad, everyone is desperate to keep alive the elderly has been mightily improved, senility continues to increase. (280)

Theo, a qualified articulate cynic condemns the evangelists of losing hope and the prophets of hateful doom. Ralph C. Wood says that, "The world will end; he agrees with T.S. Eliot in *The Hollow Men,* not with an apocalyptic bang but with an improved whimper. Between the desire and the spasm, between the potency and the existence, between the essence and the descent, Eliot wrote in 1925, falls the shadow" (281). P.D James is closer to T.S Eliot than to George Eliot. Emerson's famous saying is that when the gods go, the half gods arrive. P.D. James visualises something, far worse. Her opinion is that when God himself disappears, the demonic emerges. Yeats' terrible prophecy will come frightfully true in the Britain of 2021. The spiritually empty masses leave seculariced Christianity. They are desperate enough to turn to reactionary politics that controls the social violence.

The people have surrendered their freedom to the government. In exchange for security, they are ready to welcome despotism. Such a political system, "gives the illusion of democracy to people who no longer have the energy to care how or by whom they are governed as long as they get what the Warden has promised: freedom from fear, freedom from want, freedom from boredom"(89). Carl Inglebach is one of the members of the Council of Five. This Lenin like member serves as the philosopher of this brave new society. C.S. Lewis calls modern human beings as "trousered apes". P.D. James totally agrees with the gruesome truth of Lewis argument.

The guest workers or Sojourners are the most used and abused in James's Britain of the future. They are expected to do dirty work: "to do our dirty work, clean the sewers, clear away the rubbish, look after the incontinent, the aged" (58). The plight of the prisoners on Isle of Man is worse than the fate of the Sojourners. P.D James suggests a way out. She discloses the nature of divine rescue that reveals the springs of redemption. It is difficult for her to describe real goodness and to make virtue believable. In fiction, evil is readily amenable. Dramatically, wickedness can be depicted with searing accuracy. All good things are supposed to be small and fragile. The fallen and impure goodness can also produce evil. Theo occasionally attends church service because he is not a believer.

P.D. James explores many mysteries in this novel. The mystery of Conversion is the deepest. It can be achieved when people are transformed from rebels into self regarding and surrendering people. Theo is prompted to revolt against evil due to his own revulsion at the Quietus and the clubbing of the helpless old woman. He gradually realises what is wrong with his solitary and self- protective life, what is right about of life of mutual trust and solidarity. Theo finds it difficult to embrace Julian's faith even though his name means God-praiser. Theo is ready to die in order for Julian to live. He becomes a Christian indeed before he can confess faith in Word. He has his doubts regarding the pregnancy of Julian. He gives water to Julian asking her to drink it and be grateful.

P.D. James is not very successful when she resorts to direct allegory. Theo observes that, "we are humiliated at the very heart of our faith in ourselves. For all our knowledge, our intelligence, our power, we can no longer do what the animals do without thought. No wonder we both worship and resent them" (6). P.D. James's odd hope is that God calls for the children of men to return and to be born anew. She firmly believes the God who summons and also the God who provides. Ralph the critic, declares that, "a child is born, a son is given, and the yoke of an oppressor is broken. The frailest of all things, a baby's cry, results in radical deliverance"(288). P.D. James is gifted with extraordinary imaginative power. She promises that the morning tide of heavenly hope can rapidly rise.

Theo carries out everything that could be done to protect the new life. But fascists and rebels are reluctant to welcome the new life. The phrase 'The Children of God' suggests human potentials, divine guidance and the hope of redemption. The title 'The Children of Men' given by P.D. James is a demeaning phrase. She brings out a fall from grace, human weakness, impermanence, cruelty, violence, lust for power and in short, the darker side of human spirit. This science fiction is definitely a prophetic vision of a very near future but also in a way has a morality tale in it. Quoting from *Literary Masterpiece, and World Literature*,

> … echoes the religious story of Mary and the Infant Jesus pursued by Herod and protected by an awed band of worshippers, in this case people willing to die themselves so that mother and child can thrive. The action therein moves forward like a mystery as well, with traitors whose egos take dominance over philosophical commitments, and with a final murder that changes the future and forces a decent man to step into a power he has not wanted for the good of humankind. (2)

The mixture of hope and cynicism at the end of the novel leaves one to wonder the way in which good intentions can turn crooked in politics, as in daily life. The poem *The Hollow Men* by T.S Eliot ends with description of anticlimactic destruction, "This is the way the world ends/ Not with a bang but a whimper". P.D. James *The Children of Men* explores a dystopia that faces a similar unspectacular and silent annihilation. The Christian symbolism in *The Children of Men* is unmistakable. Ralph, the critic says that,

> The novel's final section is entitled Alpha, even as the first was called Omega. Thus has the fallen and finite course of things been reversed. In my end says Eliot of "East Coker," "is my beginning." Theodore Faron's last act, perhaps in surprise even to himself, is also a drastic new start, a return to the God who is Alpha and Omega: he makes the sign of cross. Such a finish does not evoke "the melancholy, long withdrawing roar" of Mathew Arnold's "Dover Beach," nor even the current may be fast falling toward final entropy. (288)

P.D. James seems to suggest that if faith and hope prevail, deliverance may come. Courtney McAllister in his article "The Children of Men by P.D. James, Dystopian fiction", shows his approval that,

> The Children of Men is a unique dystopia in several respects. The absence of an obvious villain is one example. There are clearly flaws in Xan's governance. However, he does not seem to be an inhuman monster or a fundamentally evil entity. For the most part, he runs the country as though it were a massive hospice. He can't "cure" his people of their infertility or their ensuing despair, so he focuses on providing some degree of pleasure and comfort. It's difficult to condemn him for adopting this approach, even though it has negative consequences – like the Quietus. (5)

People who are unable to add to the earth's population wish the human race to live on. They believe that other generations will walk through their buildings and read their books. They are convinced that there will be children to grow up in their world that they leave behind. To quote from *Literary Masterpiece, A Critical Compilation*, she has said in 1986, "we all need to believe that love is stronger than death, that the human spirit is indestructible, can surmount almost anything that fate can throw against it" (2). Her theme song is 'All you Need Is Love.' People are advised to read the novel as speculative dystopia that is uncomfortably recognisable.

P.D James' departure from the usual genre is intended to be a fable. Unfortunately the meaning is not readily communicated. Her skill as a convincing depicter of scene and character is to be appreciated and acknowledged. The critic Molly Finn, in *Commonwealth Reviews* points out that, "the numerous characters wander over a skillfully depicted landscape like so many sticks. It is too difficult to believe a redeemer will rise from the bed in the woodshed. The idea was a good one"(2). The ability to create a well-placed plot assures her that her dystopian novel is as exciting as her crime stories. There are various aspects concerning the protagonists in the dystopian novel. The suppression of free will and attitude of the authorities are the main reasons for the revolt of the main protagonist. So there is a threat to the stability of the state. The authorities try to gain the control of their personality. They deprive the protagonists of their independent thoughts.

The heroes face either success or failure at the end. Some of them are murdered. Some of them are forced to commit suicide. Invariably all the protagonists experience the fear of punishment, humiliation or advanced technology. The passivity, a common future of dystopian society is the most significant fear. A typical trait within the novel is anxiety about the future. The heroes of the dystopian novels fight for the independence and live with the hope. Their situations may seem to be hopeless but they trust in better future. A comparative study of protagonists in P.D. James's *The Children of Men* and Shakespeare's *King Lear* provides an accurate description of a real hero. Motivated by various factors both of them go through life- changing experiences. Many similarities are there, including their unwillingness to maintain power and to take responsibilities. The passivism of Theo till his visit to the Quietus is shocking. King Lear is so passive that he surrenders all his power to his daughters.

T.S. Eliot's *The Wasteland* and P.D. James *The Children of Men* depict the universal theme, namely the natural and spiritual rebirth. Without hope, people are nothing more than a handful of dust. To quote T.S. Eliot, from his modern epic poem *The Wasteland*, "I will show you fear in a handful of dust" (64). The Fisher king is a ruler of the barren wasteland. It has been plagued by disease. The women are infertile in the land of Fisher king. In *The Children of Men*, men are infertile and the infertility tests are compulsory. Theo comes to be a perfect modern embodiment. The birth of the baby boy revives his hope for a better future and his faith is gradually rekindled. Towards the end T.S Eliot's Fisher king repeats the word "Shantih Shantih Shantih" which means peace and understanding.

The critic Brad Hooper in the website, 'Infertility book. Com' says that, "All of James' ability to draw characters in full dimension and to keep a plot well paced is in evidence. Still, the world and issues she's created here seem redundant--not unlike what's been done before by many other writers." P.D. James novel draws a mystic breath. The satire in the bleak end of the novel point out that this is the future of humanity: to embrace the chance of origin by what may be seen as imperfect but essentially, human. Theo finds this love and passion for life through Julian. It is Julian who is passionate and religious and has taught him to see beauty even in ordinary things. Even when Theo learns the truth that Luke, the priest is the father of the child and not Rolf her husband, he does not hate her. He readily joins their escape attempt from the government. Xan goes after them when he finds out from Rolf about Julian's pregnancy. Julian insists that the birth of her baby should take place away from the public eye. Theo is naturally worried about the safety of Julian and the child. When they have reached the safety of forest, Theo "could understand now her obstinate choice and it seemed to him, sitting in this peace and quietness, to be both right and reasonable" (225).

P.D James uses formal and long winded language. She succeeds in creating a feeling of being a classic and timeless piece of writing. As she has to convey a serious message, this language has served the purpose. She has given more importance to language and meaning than to the events. Modern style is suitable to convey a light hearted mood. James style is apt for describing a man's inner struggle. The majority of the characters happen to be highly intelligent, Theo the professor and historian, the Warden of England, Luke the priest and the council. This novel has straight forward plots with many flash backs. It gives an insight to his character and a connection and an understanding of his action. When the character is established, the pace of the novel quickens. The flashback in his diary, narrates Theo's journey to love and meaning in life.

Julian's unexpected pregnancy and the birth of the baby boy shoot a burst of hope for both Theo and human kind. She said: "See, you have a son,' and laughed. It seemed to Theo that the decrepit shed rang with her joyful and triumphant voice. He looked down at Julian's outstretched arms and transfigured face, then turned away. The joy was almost too much for him to bear". (228)

Theo has realised that it will be hailed as a miracle birth. Julian has a different kind of hope. She is hopeful of the future. Others can lead a normal life with her son. The triumph of "hope over hopelessness" is beautifully described by P.D James. She is known for her religious notion. But she is clever enough to find a way of connecting new life and new hope with plot and characters. P.D. James' fans are usually prepared for murder mysteries. They are used to a well knit plot, the suspense and the excitement of chase. Contrary to their expectations, James in her only dystopian novel, addresses different problems existing in futuristic world. She deals different aspects efficiently, such as a sterility of body and spirit, leading the list. It is really long as she tackles the destruction of society, questions of individual and governmental power, religious belief, love and redemption. It is really a harrowing experience for England and human race to survive this state of affairs. Quoting from *Kiruku Reviews*, "The departure from her usual former is brilliantly conceived the note of sad mortality so powerfully sustained that James's benediction of hope is almost unbearable."

P. D James has a meticulous eye for tiny but significant details. It coexists with her soaring imagination. She imagines a future of children and invites the readers also to imagine so. Her imagination is convincing and as well as frightening. She deals with the suppressed, mythical side of human nature. *The Children of Men* is certainly arresting.

William Murchison in his *Children of Men: Read the Book!* talks about her explanation of experience before writing her dystopian novel:

> dealing with the dramatic and so far unexplained fall in the fertility rate of Western man." She wondered: What if the human races were "struck by a universal infertility"? She saw a gradual falling away of hope and expectation; the replacement of adventure by ruin; a world steadily running downhill, crumbling to the touch, "all hope and ambition lost forever, the meaning of life itself quite gone. (23)

Some people argue that *Children of Men* is of highest calibre among the dystopian fiction. It is beautifully written, profound and catches attention. Some critics are of the feeling that it can be placed along with the towering achievements of Huxley, Orwell and Bradhery. *The Children of Men* can be described as biting godless, self absorbed culture. She uses irony when she points out that the world of 2021 is dying, because it wants pleasure without the 'risk' of children. Sex has become the least important of man's sensory pleasure. It is noteworthy that P.D. James makes a striking and pervasive use of Christian imagery. Her narrative bears a marked resemblance to the nativity story. P.D. James' dystopian novel is deeply an ideological novel, tackling with theological questions. It may be termed as a Christian novel, preachy and Bible thumping. P.D James weaves Christian ideas into the story in seamless and in an artful manner.

The concern of the novelist towards the society and mankind is well brought out. She is worried about the mother earth becoming sterile on the whole. If the fertility rate of the humans falls down steadily in a frightful manner then the future of them is going to be a big question mark. The hollowness once formed cannot be easily filled up. The writer feels that it is her moral duty to pull out the society from sinking into the quick sand. She, as a writer is able to is visualise the fearful futuristic society which will one day become totally impotent. As such, the advent of science has its monstrous growth and extended its horrible tentacles all over. Humans are not only caught in the cruel clutches but slowly seem to perish in themselves. The writer wants to warn the people of the forthcoming danger and come to an awakening. The approaching hayard is no ordinary one. If not given a proper watch over it, in no time it will eat up the society.

P.D James does not think that her job is over by creating awareness among the people of the dystopian effect. She does not stop with the exposures of the problem alone. In this novel, she has also highlighted a ray of hope. Every dark cloud has a silver lining and after every dark night comes a bright day. So, any problem or disaster for that matter, when well analysed will definitely have a solution. Thus, the novelist not only talks about the preventive measures but also about the after methods to overcome it. Love and affection play a dominant role to help one to see the dawn of the day. The frightful sterile future of mankind has indeed covered like a canopy over their existence. It exhibits darkness everywhere and man is groping in the dark for at least a thin streak of light so as to overcome his fear. The novelist underlines the fact that the very light which would eradicate the grief and fear of the mankind is nothing but caring love which in then would head to many beautiful and happy openings. Man should realise the importance of conjugal love which would give life to the sterility. The birth will for sure mark a new beginning.

CONCLUSION

Sir Thomas More has depicted *Utopia* as "a small island, harbouring a homogeneous, egalitarian and pacifistic city state in which social virtues prevail. Evils, such as perversity and misery are absent, possibly explaining why utopia has few laws and no lawyers". (10) Such a vision and depiction of an ideal society is extremely good. But in reality, it is impossible to achieve one like it. It can never exist in real life, but only in dreams. Such an ideally, perfect place can be imagined in its social, political and moral aspects. Huxley in *Contemporary Literary Criticism* points out the aim of establishing an utopian society:

> Huxley's comprehensive scientific knowledge with satire of contemporary society to project a future totalitarian state based on values and trends of the modern world. Examining the fate of the individual in a technologically advanced society, Huxley critizes the result of unchecked scientific achievement, intense social conditioning and single minded pursuit of pleasure, which together could turn humans "into a kind of uniformity." Regarding the aim of establishing a utopian society, Huxley stated: "anyone who believes that there is some magical shortcut out of man's chronologically tragic situation is inviting either violent catastrophe through an ideological crusade or else a slower but equally sure disaster through the creation of a brave new world". (1)

More has successfully depicted the state of Utopia. According to him it is a place where everyone enjoys the freedom of speech. It is not a crime to express one's own opinion. More's *Utopia*, points out that "tolerance is a necessary of any ideal state" (133).

Marx and Engels in *The Communist Manifesto,* (1967) have warned and defined utopia as "as a fantastic picture of future society, painted at a time when the proletariat is still in a very undeveloped state and has but a fantastic conception of its own passion"(116). Only the human being have the ability to draw of a better or worse life. Theshidies of nature (science) leads to transformation of nature (technology). Some of the best thinkers have created imaginative works called utopia and dystopias, which are sometimes called as anti-utopia. These great thinkers and explorers of science, technology and ethics have frightened and enlightened the people. Plato's classic utopia narrates the escape of hero's escape from the allegorical cave of shadows in *The Republic* (360).

Northrop Frye in his, *Anatomy of Criticism,* brings out the distinction between imaginary and imaginative. First he asserts that, "utopian thought is imaginative". He observes that, "…the word imaginative refer to hypothetical construction, like those of literature on mathematics... The word imaginary refers something that does not exist."(193-195) More's island is a new 'no place' that people can hold in their hands and in their minds; it is imaginative, not imaginary. Fortunati and Trousson in *Dictionary of Literary Dystopia* points out that More's *Utopia* is, "a bewildering mixture of reality and fiction".(15) The religion is the evidence of free will in utopia. Utopian citizens have the choice to select belief and worship. They have independence and have the chance to maintain their individuality . But the utopian law does not allow laziness. Even the utopians are supposed to follow certain rules. They are not allowed to indulge in useless activities. According to More the man, the utopian laws and customs "were really absurd… utopia depicts, not a perfect… (110). More's utopians have no desire for violence and war; there is no need for the ruler for any force or war since the citizens live in peace and mutual solidarity. In general, "the utopians detest war thing" (51).

Andrew Hammond in his *Utopia and Dystopia* points out that, "Utopia depicts not perfect social, legal and political system, but instead a complex debate, enriched by human, between More's earned political realism of low expectation and his cautious optimism of higher desires for society" (3). More himself accepts that the road to utopia is paved with unclear intentions. Utopianism consists of three facts: a liberty tradition, an ideology and a tradition of communal living and organizations. In other words utopianism is secular perfectibility. Even though utopia is defined as the portrayal of the perfect society, More does not portray this perfection. People are aware of the existence of crime, welfare and folly; anti-utopia is a misinterpretation of the concept of utopia, which mistakes the earthly for the divine. Gregory Claeys, in his article "Three Variants on the concept of Dystopia" published in *Dystopia(n) Matters on the Page on Screen, on Stage* says that, "If the garden of Eden is the key model for the original Westernn , Judaeo Christian utopian tradition, expulsion from it would possibly imply that subsequent human life is itself dystopian"(18).

Utopia is like a mathematical equation. It succeeds in achieving an imaginative order. It not only accounts for all doubts but it also solves. Dystopia, a later genre has been coined in the year 1947. It picturises a hypothetical place, a society on situation. The conditions and the quality of life are extremely bad due to deprivation, oppression or terror. After the period of World War II, this genre has become popular. It has gained more popularity in the twentieth century due to the horror of wars, totalitarian regimes or anxiety about the nuclear threat. Krishan Kumar in *Utopia and Anti-Utopia in Modern Times*, traces the general characteristic of dystopia and stresses the idea that,

> The earliest forms of utopia seem to have been satires on the rationalist and scientific utopias of More and Bacon" the reason why "why it is mainly in the twentieth century that dystopia truly comes into its own", Kumar explains, is that its targets, right from the beginning, have been the 'grand narratives' of modernity- reason and revolution, science and socialism the idea of progress and the faith and future and most of these elements only really spread on a significant scale in the latter part of the nineteenth century. (380-81)

Dystopia differs from that of utopia. It is supposed to be an invent, mirror negative version of utopia. Dystopia is a much younger concept, dating only from the later nineteenth century. It may be considered as the essence of utopia than being the negation of utopia. One may consider a person as a freedom fighter. The same person may be described as a terrorist. In the same way one person's utopia is another's dystopia. Gregory Claey's in his article "Three Variants on the Concept of Dystopia" gives three definitions of dystopia:

> The first definition can be termed as the 'identity' definition. The greatest tragedy of modernity is pursuit of the secular millennium. The second definition of dystopia is the perversion of the former. The third definition remarks 'dystopia' from More's tradition in general. In short dystopia is a broad and diverse tradition. (17)

Heaven and Garden of Eden remain prototypes of dystopia. Hell performs the same role for dystopia. The dystopian societies are controlled and influenced by the elite powers. The citizens living in the dystopian world become an easy prey and offer no resistance at all. So the dystopian society does not have space for free will, justice or peaceful life. Gottlieb in *Utopian Thought in the Western World* claims: "the individual has become a victim experiencing loss of control over his or her destiny in the face of monstrous, superhuman force" (11).

Dystopian literature has gained its popularity and prominence due to certain accidents. Modern literature people continue to read negative texts and dystopian novels. Literature of this period especially dystopian portrays a skeptical attitude towards science and technological progress and it has described frightful visions of the world controlled by machines. Dystopia is supposed to be the darkest form of government. Monarchy is one of the two types of dystopia. A monarch, a king or queen is more or less a dictator who makes every decision. He has absolute control over the citizens. Communistic government, not a governing body is just the opposite of monarchy. In many ways the two types are seemingly alike. Monarchy is bad but communism is also bad. It is the worst kind of government, being watched all the time with no freedom and democracy, only mind games.

Dystopia is an utopia gone wrong; classless, moneyless and common ownership. Everyone owns everything which is really horrible because no one has any personal property. It is a horrible concept and is really deceptive. These two types of dystopia, monarchies and communism fall apart and result in revolutions but not before the death of millions of innocent people. They are severely crushed, for, a brutal force is applied effectively to stop their resistance and revolts. Societies in the past have experienced a change of regime mainly under totalitarian rule. According to Seligman's theory of positive psychology,

> people should concentrate on their perspectives for the future and utilize all their strengths in achieving personal satisfaction. However, his observations do not reject the importance of the past. Knowing one's self is the basis of practicing "positive psychology." And this knowledge could only arise from the knowledge of one's past and traditions. (178)

Dystopian society is carved by manipulation of the society. People have longed for a perfect society where everyone is happy and prosperous. They have searched for such a society for many decades. Novelists and movies have tried to help the people to explore and experience, by depicting an utopian world. Great thinkers and writers with realistic approach have succeeded in imagining and creating a creation of a counter genre of utopia, namely dystopia. Dystopian novelists like Huxley and Orwell are convinced that the manipulation of human mind and human emotion will lead to dystopian future. The society is approaching a dystopian culture where the government has full control over their thoughts and lives. Raffaella Baccolni in the article "The Persist ant of Hope in Dystopian Science Fiction"in *Correspondents Abroad* mentions that dystopia, "is traditionally a bleak, depressing genre with no space life for hope in the story" (520).

Huxley's message in his novel *Brave New World* warns about the dangers of totalitarian regimes. They dominate the population leaving no space for individuality and freedom. It is an effective warning for the generations to come. *Brave New World* is regarded as a classic examination of modern values. Critics consider Huxley's dystopia as a satire; it is a mockery of the scientific and social progress. Jerry W. Carlson in *Dictionary of Literary Biography* has stated that in *Brave New World* Huxley explores "the... by problem of how modern mass society could destroy the values of individualism by accepting a false belief in perfection standardization..." (46). The novel is indeed a remarkable journey into the future. Dusterhoff , Guynn, , Patterson and , Shaw, together have written in *Huxley's Brave New World :A Study Of Dehumanization.*

> ...wherein mankind is dehumanized by the progress and misuse of technology to the point where society is a laboratory produced race of beings who are clones devoid of identity only able to worship the three things they have been preconditioned to love: "Henry Ford, their idol; Soma, a wonder drug; and sex. (1)

When Huxley published this dystopian novel certain concepts are not realities. But they are indeed very frightening concepts. Babies conceived in the laboratory, gene splicing, reproduction and wonder drugs to relieve psychic pain have been imagined scientific developments, during the time of Huxley but they have become real now. The publishers have described the novel as "witty and wickedly satirical". Ford is substituted for God. John the Savage has grown up in a very confused state. He is abandoned by his mother the child of a civilized woman. He has learned to value heroism, self discipline and chastity. He finds it difficult to give up all the values. He is in trouble and is arrested. Margaret Cheney Dawson in *Huxley Turns Propagandist*, mentions that,

> There follow a dialogue that contains the meat of the matter, during John pleads for the "right to be unhappy" and protests against "getting rid of everything unpleasant instead learning to put up with it". Both arguments controller meets with commendable placidity, while showing John out the door. The unhappy Savage retires to seclusion and eventually to suicide and then at very end, after all the sound and fury , Mr. Huxley relents for a moment and gives us a few plangent phrases in which lie the only echo of his former work, the only whisper of better things to come.(5)

Huxley's most successful novel describes in detail, the drug abuse. Fictional and real drugs figure prominently. He makes a great effort of his fictional mokstia medicine. He condemns recreational drug abuse anti-intellectualism, mindless popular eutoinment sexual promiscuity, materialism and enforced race and class equality. John Hickman in

"When Science Fiction Writers Used Fictional Drugs: Rise and Fall of the Twentieth-Century Drug Dystopia" says that,

> Mustapha Mond, Resident Controller of Western Europe and one of the World State's ten ruling controllers, explains: "God isn't compatible with machinery and universal happiness. You must make your choice. Our civilization has chosen machinery and medicine and happiness" The native of this dystopia are the contemptibly shallow, spiritually, empty products of modernity. Their use of recreational drug soma is one of several aspects of dehumanization made possible by the scientific expertise wielded by amoral elites. (4)

In his Foreword Huxley, throws light on the theme of *Brave New World* by pointing out that,

> …The theme *of Brave New World* is not an advancement of science as such; it is advancement of science as it affects human individuals… The only scientific advances to be specifically described are those involving the application to human beings, of the results of future research in biology, physiology and psychology…(ii)

Huxley who happens to be an intellectual artist does not use his novel merely as a vehicle of debate. *Brave New World* portrays a society where aging does not exist for the "scare mongering prophets of doom, a life of unremitting bliss is not nearly as bad as it sounds" (4). The exchange between Savage and Controller goes like the, in the novel,

> 'But I like the inconveniences.'

> 'We don't,' said the Controller. 'We prefer to do things comfortably.'
> 'But I don't want comfort. I want God, I want poetry, I want real danger, I want freedom, I want goodness, I want sin.'
> 'In fact,' said Mustapha Mond, "you're claiming the right to be unhappy.'
> 'Not to mention the right to grow old and ugly and impotent; the right to have syphilis and cancer; the right to have too little to eat; the right to be lousy; the right to live in constant apprehension of what may happen tomorrow; the right to catch typhoid; the right to be tortured by unspeakable pains of every kind.' There was a long silence.
> 'I claim them all,' said the Savage at last.
> Mustapha Mond shrugged his shoulders. 'You're welcome,' he said. (212)

John the Savage is a meaningful and significant character, compared to the clones of *Brave New World.* He is repelled by the sexual license of the new world. He has an aversion for women who make advances. He wants women to love rather than merely make love to. Obviously the Savage remains a lone wolf in the techno dictated society. Huxley opts for the blending of scientific knowledge and religious wisdom to achieve a blissful existence. Huxley does not totally condemn drugs. The effects of soma are described as "euphoric, narcotic, pleasantly halluchant. It offers an escape from the reality, free from unpleasant physical side effects" (46). Many novelists have described about drug abuse in their fictions. The intake of drugs is mainly because of human inability to resist the trails and tribulation of life. But what has to be taken as a small dose of medicine soon leads them to a sort of addiction and then the disastrous consequences.

Huxley offers fictional drugs that reinforce what is dystopia in their societies. Novels describing dystopian societies are common. The long list of dystopian novels present oppressive political regimes. But drug dystopias are rare. Science fiction has become a vehicle for promoting drug use in 1975. Naming one of his fictional drugs, appears to be a real homage to Aldous Huxley. In his 1975 report written for the National Institute of Drug Abuse, the science fiction author Robert Silverberg in "Drug themes in Science Fiction," has defined the genre as "branch of fantasy which engages in imaginative speculation about the impact of technology on human society"(3). Drug have been used as both medicine and recreation in every human society. New drugs have been developed and introduced in rapid pace. It has its benefits and challenges. The novelist warns about the utility of pharmacology to tyranny. Several specific social evils, described in the novels continue to be relevant.

Huxley's *Brave New World* is rightly called a dystopian novel. It signals the start of a new era. It is an era of enlightened individuals versus the termite ideal. The period of unchallenged individualism and comfortable humanitarianism is once for all over. *Brave New World* anticipates and tries to see beyond the new. Huxley's novel is a problematic one. Satirical techniques, somewhat peculiar are handled by Huxley. Realism is the most significant characteristic of the novel. Critics have considered it, as a work in, the tradition of utopia and dystopian literature. To conclude, John Colmer in *Utopian Fantasy*, pays a fitting tribute to Huxley by saying that, "Huxley, by carrying twentieth-century trends to their logical conclusion and by clever parodies of modern social rituals, makes us feel the pressing relevance of *Brave New World* (170).

George Orwell, the British novelist has felt himself responsible in the face of history, for moral awareness and social justice. In his generation, he only has successfully fathomed the simplification of his time. In his own words he only manages to remain an "outside whale" as a person and as a novelist, 'he loved the past, hated the present and dreaded the future'. In order to frighten the people into a painful recognition of the dangers that threaten their very existence, Orwell has written the novel *Nineteen Eighty – Four* a nightmarish vision of the future. Irving How, in his article "Orwell: History as Nightmare" published in *Politics and the Novel* says,

> … *Nineteen Eighty –Four* is a novel about the future that is, it is in a sense a fantasy, but in the form of a naturalistic novel… it is intended as show up of the perversion to which a central economy is liable, and which have already been partly realized in communism and fascisms… totalitarian ideas have taken to root in the minds of intellectual everywhere, and I have tried to draw these ideas out their logical consequence... (235)

Orwell in his 'Orwellian Dystopia' *Nineteen Eighty –Four* crafts a dark, realistic atmosphere of a communist post World War II super country. A third person narration of a realistic character depicts a deceptive totalitarian government. This government manipulates historical records to maintain power and keeps secret surveillance. The major influence for this novel is Jonathan Swift's *Gulliver's Travels*. When there is a dishonest and secretive society in power, one can be assured of the arrival of the rebels within the society. It is vulnerable and unstable. An overdose of violence and lack of freedom results in the development of rebels. When a fair treatment is not meted out to the citizens, they go against rules and regulations. In *Nineteen Eighty –Four* Winston Smith and Julia are considered to be the rebels. The Big brother, the god like ruler of Oceania, is meant for worship and not for hatred. Winston Smith has written, 'down with Big brother', over and over in his diary. It is a crime to have a bad thought about him. The offence is called face crime, deserving a punishment,

> it was terribly dangerous to let your thoughts wander when you where in any public place or within the range of a telescreen. The smallest thing could give you away. A nervous tic, an unconscious look of anxiety, a habit of muttering to yourself- anything that carried with it the suggestion of abnormally or living something to hide. (56)

Even thoughts against the ruling party are prohibited. But Smith commits thought crime. He dares to fight for power. He is forced to endure mental and physical hardship. Gradually he realises the truth about Big Brother and even manages to fall in love with Julia, another rebel and partner in crime. Winston Smith who is ahead of his time is not stupid. As his first act of rebellion, he maintains a diary of his thought crime. He knows the terrible consequences and the punishment namely death. He notes down the number of people, who have disappeared over the years without a trace:

> O'Brien, a sophisticated member of the Inner Party, characterise the restrictions, Winston is obliged to undergo for the sake of disobedience. Everything that you have undergone since you have been in our hands-all

> that will continue, and worse. The espionage, the betrayals, the arrests, the tortures, the executions, the disappearance will never cease.(242)

Orwell often repeats and adopts for *Nineteen Eighty –Four* an idea. The idea is that in the end the Party would announce that two and two make five and one would have to believe it. Orwell's review of Bertrand Russell's "Symptoms of Orwell's 1984" in *Portraits from Memory*, book on power, "It is quite possible that we are descending into an age in which two and two will make five when the leader says so. Mr Russell points out that the huge system of organised lying upon which the dictator depend, keeps their followers out of contact with reality" (376). For Winston, the psychological effect of political oppression, is the loss of childhood memories. The critics highlight a feature of the novel namely the psychological affinity between Winston and O'Brien.

In the novel *Nineteen Eighty –Four*, the society is divided into four different sections. At the top of the social pyramid is Big Brother, followed by the Inner party. Then comes the Outer Party. Proles occupy the last level which represents eighty five percent of the whole population. This social pyramid is the typical pattern of dystopian literature. Big Brother who is watching everyone occupies the top spot. Oceania, owned by the Inner Party, consists of the higher class people. They enjoy certain privileges like good food, servants and watching telescreen. The Inner Party leads a very good and luxurious life. Outer party lives a completely opposite one; no privacy, constant monitoring by telescreens, use of fake masks and yielding and obeying each and every command of the government. Orwell has intended his novel as a commentary on the

Soviet threat. He indicates his intention in portraying the totalitarian system, the oppressive environment of London and the demoralising effect upon the individual,

> Orwell indicates that he will weave together the portrayal of the totalitarian system, older concerns such as the oppressive government of London, and demoralizing effect upon the individual he begins with "the system of organizing lying," "leader worship, etc" and "the swindle of Bakerism and Ingsoc" to describe a protagonist beset by "the nightmare feeling caused by the disappearance of objective truth," "his feeling of being the last man and doubts of own sanity". (29)

Orwell always maintains a general conception of a totalitarian system which is not tied to a specific country or ideology. He is a profoundly important and one of the influntical political novelists of the West. The combination of *Nineteen Eighty-Four* and Cold war has turned the figure of Orwell from author to a personality and to a 'myth'. Smith who is under the constant observation of the State is naturally depressed. The Ministry of Truth is specilised in propaganda where as Ministry of Love maintains order through detainment and torture. The Ministry of Peace fights wars and finally the Ministry of Plenty has false claims of economic prosperity. This dark irony is used by Orwell throughout the novel. During Two Minute Hate, Winston switches from loathing to adoration of the "invicible, fearless protector, Big Brother" (151). There is degradation in the domestic life by the state.

In order to retain his knowledge, Winston Smith has to predicate "double think". He must "be conscious of complete truthfulness while telling carefully constructed lies" (31). Double think gives way to the erasure of memory. Towards the end, Winston Smith gazes up at the enormous portrait of the telescreen. He realises that he loves Big Brother. He gives up his memory. Once again he accepts the orders and truth of the State/ Party. He gives up resistance for the sake of contentment. Orwell is concerned about a 'machine' society. Due to the rapid technological development, this is applicable to men and communist system. The unifying image in *Nineteen Eighty-Four* is Big Brother, the leader of Oceania. Smith's quest for memory for his history, for love and for inner peace is represented by the image of the golden country. The icon image of Big Brother is embedded in the culture. Orwell makes a political statement to warn the people. The novelist is successful in painting a totalitarian society where the people are forced to live in, a kind of hysteria. Isaac Deutscher in *Heretics and Renegades and Other Essays* describes, *Nineteen Eighty-Four* as "a kind of ideological weapon in the cold war"(172).

The novel revolves around three main characters: Winston Smith, lady love Julia, and O'Brien. O'Brien happens to be an official in the inner party. Winston Smith has been described as an extension of Orwell and his character is well defined. Julia can be regarded as a foil to her lover Smith and his political and personal hopes and fears. O'Brien happens to be an embodiment of Smith's complex attraction and rebellion against oppressive and tyrannical state. Winston Smith is transformed from a coward, a cipher doing his tiresome work for the state into a man who dares to hope. He starts this change with reluctance but his association with Julia, quickens his development. It does not mean that he is becoming an optimistic man. The Ministry of Love sees to it that his transformation is undone. His phobias, such as fear of rats, the recovery of childhood memory end not with pleasure but with horrific realisation.

One of Huxley's character's outlook is that, "we don't want to change is a menace to stability" (198). It is clear that the government determines the social class and manipulates. Huxley issues a clean statement, "there will never be social stability without individual stability". Orwell's concept of Doublethink, Newspeak, and Big Brother bring out his fear of the future. Harold Rosenberg in *The Tradition of the New* states,

> the tone of the post-war imagination was set by Orwell's 1984: since the appearance of that work, (the theme of) the "dehumanized collective" haunts our thoughts. Orwell's unique contribution to English passionate commitment, a radical sincerity and an ethic of responsibility that ultimately transcend his defeated heroes.(157)

Writers of science fiction have analysed Orwell's irony, parody, prophecy, psychology, masochism and theory of language. Orwell's fear of the future and what he has called 'the mysticism of cruelty has been discussed by the critics.

Dystopian novels have a rich history and include works such as Jonathan Swift's eighteenth century classic, *Gulliver's Travels.* The dystopian novels have become prevalent and popular after World War II. Burgess is an able satirist. Robert K. Morris in his article "The Bitter Fruits of Freedom," published in *The Consolations of Ambiguity,* mentions that, "...Like all good satirists', Burgess lashes out with savage indignation at stupidity and blind error and lacerates our disastrous pretensions at solving human problem at the expense of human beings…" (55). The major theme of *A Clockwork Orange* is the ability of the individual to make choice. Burgess is of the opinion that destroying the ability to choose evil, destroys the capacity to choose good. *A Clockwork Orange* explores the ideas of good and evil by asking what it means to be human. The state is against the liberties of the individual. The relationship between the state and individual in a society has deteriorated. The state tries to control the individual through regulation, law and brutal force. When the state enjoys so much power, naturally it crushes the individuals. Liberties of freedom of speech and expression is lost to a large extent.

Burgess considers an evil Alex as a human. So an Alex, who has been programmed to deny his own nature is preferable to the writer. At one point F.Alexander tells to Alex,

> They have turned you into something other than a human being. You have no power of choice any longer. You are committed to socially acceptable acts, a little machine capable only of good." Later, he adds, "The essential intention [of the Ludovico Technique] is the real sin. A man who cannot choose ceases to be a man." The repetition of Alex's phrase "What's it going to be then, eh?". (174-175)

He happens to be an ultra violent, charming rapist, killer and a fifteen year old thief. The thematic elements and the style of the novel have received favourable reviews. The 1987 American editor carries a blurb from *Time Magazine* that states, 'Anthony Burgess has written what looks like a nasty little shock, but is really a rare thing in English letters, a philosophical novel'. Alex makes a compelling anti-hero. In Anthony Burgess, Samuel Coale notes that Burgess has made Alex a sympathtic character. He is gifted with an artistic consciousness. He dresses up well and loves classical music, especially Beethovan. Colae in his book *Anthony Burgess* observes:

> There are, then, at least two Alex's confronting the reader. Is he merely a clockwork automaton, a creature of his mechanized society, whose violence is merely an extension of his own boredom and sense of worthlessness? Or is he, in fact, better than his clockwork society, an artistic and intelligent person? His appreciation of music emphasizes this dichotomy (91).

Alex and his droogs engage in acts of extreme violence. Innocent citizens and other gangs are attacked by them. Alex refers to himself as 'your humble narrator' or a 'handsome young narrator'. The readers are shocked and intrigued by Alex's brutality. This stream of consciousness novel discusses the struggle between good and evil. The novelist also focuses on the theme of youth versus old age and illusion versus reality. Alex enjoys unlimited free will that he can exercise. There is no definitive state control to keep these ultraviolent groups in line. Alex declares, "A man who cannot choose ceases to be a man" (175). This free will helps them to get away with things or twist the system. This anti-utopian novel describes an imminent future in a stately supervised country.

Alex revolts against the state using violence and ends up in prison. In the end, he is turned into a harmless subject without free will, incapable of committing any crime. Anthony Burgess seems to criticise the state on one side and on the other side the persons and groups who opposed it.

A Clockwork Orange is considered to be one of the most experimental, original and controversial novels of the twentieth century. This compelling work of literature is known for its in depth study in linguistics. Anthony Burgess who happens to be an established linguist uses his novel to explore different languages and combines them to create Nadast, the language of the youth. It comes from the Russian words nadast, a suffix for the teenage numbers. It is made up mainly of Russian and British slang. Words from Malay, German, French, Arabi and Gypsy are borrowed and utlised. Nadast is the primary of language even though not of the exclusive one. The novelist clarifies that he uses it to create a literary adventure. Anthony Burgess in his Foreword to *A Clockwork Orange Resucked* describes that,

> The title 'A Clockwork Orange' is derived from several sources. Used in old London slang, one might say someone is "as queer as a clockwork orange". In Nadsat, "orange" means "man" (which is derived from the Malay word "orang," meaning "man"), so a clockwork orange would be a man moving without pause or thought, as a clockwork . Burgess says of the title, "I mean it to stand for the application of a mechanistic morality to a living organism oozing with juice and sweetness. After the state reforms

> him, the novel's hero and narrator Alex becomes a clockwork orange, a man working as a machine. (x)

Nadast seems to require freewill. Lack of government intervention and a possible misuse of power are clearly apparent. It shows that it is not a governing society but a correcting one when the time comes to it. In this degenerated society Alex and his droogs use "cancer" to mean cigarettes and "sinny" for cinema. It highlights the sardonic nature of the novel. Alex lives in a society which lacks individualism and opposition. The government is very strict. The ordinary citizens are deceived and confused. Television and drugs play a major role and people do not read books and newspaper. They have rarely visited theatres and cinemas. The totalitarian state has succeeded in preventing the normal subjects from thinking.

Burgess advises that people should not trust the state. His hero Alex also suspects the state. Although he acts violently, it is only to satisfy his desires. But in reality they are his expressions of distrust against the well organized state. The failure of the state is the reason for Alex, to be a cruel creature. The oppression of a police state and its powerful control, force the youth to indulge in illegal brutality. One of the officers who is interrogating Alex points out that they "know the law, too… but knowing the law isn't everything" (75). In dystopian novels scientific progress is used mainly for the importance of state control or brain washing methods. It is called the Ludovica technique in *A Clockwork Orange*. It is a chemical and visual treatment.

The reader is fascinated by the Nadast language and is used to it before the end of the first chapter. In the beginning, it has appeared to be a barrier to communication. Later on it becomes a device that enchances the narrative. A.A DeVitis an American critic and educator interprets *A Clockwork Orange* as a bleak comedy and he illustrates it in "England, Education, and the Future, in *Anthony Burgess"*:

> The activities of Alex and his 'droogs' become more terrifying, while, ironically, the language become more poetical. Phrases like "Being sore athirst, my brothers," "They know not what they mom gave me tried little smech, to these fruit of my womb my only son sort of," by their very incongruity with the activities being described, lend a note of poetic intensity to the narrative that contrasts with the nightmare horror of the action... (100)

Ludovic technique is a name, not chosen at random by Burgess. It is a treatment given to Alex. After his capture, he is brutally treated by the police. In the prison Alex kicks a cell mate to death. He is chosen as the first experiment in conditioned relax rehabilitation for this violent action. Nearly for fifteen days, he is forced to take an injection with a drug. Added to this he is shown films of sadistic violence. It is horrible and is accompanied by symphonic music. This reformatory program is presented in a radicalised form as Ludovico technique. This is supposed to be the spine of the novel. After undergoing this reprogramming and humiliating presentation of it, Alex is released from the prison. It has left him as a machine, incapable of own voluntary actions. The critic Hymn, in "Anthony Burgess' Clockwork Orange", points out that,

> the writer, strangely suggests that the moral choice by science. Burgess appears to be saying Alex is only a "clockwork orange," something mechanical that appears organic. Free to will, even if he will to sin, Alex is capable of salvation. But perhaps this is to confine Burgess' ironies and ambiguities within simple orthodoxy. Alex always was a clockwork orange, a machine for mechanical violence far below that level of choice, and his dreary socialist England is a giant clockwork orange. (661-62)

This technique evokes a number of reaction in Alex. It turns him to a nonviolent, non aggressive and respectful according to the code of the society. Burgess wants to encourage a comparison between Alex's brutality and society's Anthony Burgess' society. Carol Di, in *Translantic Review* says, "The violence in the book is really more to show what the state can do with it" (2). Alex is punished and his free will is removed. But he is made to believe that he is in control of his own body. It proves the ultimate power of the state. The citizens can never escape the confines of the dominant rulers. Irony is used through out the novel. Irony, dark humour, repetition and word play are constantly, identified. Alex's description of violence is not only a repeated example of irony. When Alex is taking the treatment, the doctors and nurses call the drugs that will destroy Alex's life as vitamins. The treatment that is given to Alex is ironic. The reason for forcing the treatment is more ironic. In order to condition him from his habit of terrorizing people, the state terrorises Alex. Burgess has said in the novel, "Juvenile delinquents destroy the state peace, mature delinquents mature delinquents the human race" (19).

In order to add humour to dialogues and the serious situations in his satirical novel, Burgess plays with puns. Although Dim lacks commonsense his friends tolerate him for his physical strength. Alex always refers Dim as, "Dim the dim" (12). Whenever he mentions the minister of the interior, he calls him, "the minister of the interior or inferior" (84). Burgess uses metaphors and similes too. Recalling the words of Alex from the novel, "There I was dancing about with my britva like I might be a barber on board a ship on a very rough sea, trying to get in at him, a few fair slashes on his nuclear oily listo" (16). The primary aim of the state is, to deny Alex a free moral choice. The gates of heaven will open for Alex. The sound of music sickens him though music is a figure of celestial bliss. Julian Mitchell, an English novelist, playwright and critic, in his "Horrorshow on Amis Avenue," says that, "…finds himself the victim of entire world, at the mercy of policeman, old professor and politicians. His responses are no longer his own…" (661-62).

A Clockwork Orange deals with an important theme, youth versus old age. It shows lawless youngsters taking over the society. Alex and his droogs attack an old woman and old man. Towards the end, Alex undergoes a total change after the brainwashing treatment. Now it is the turn of the old man who beats Alex with their canes and wheelchairs. Alex, his freedom taken away from him, is unable to defend himself. The older generation has succeeded in getting back their nation. Another prevalent theme in the novel is illusion versus reality. Alex's reality as a human being is over once for all. The state has successfully put an end to his illusions. Alex, has lost his visionary abilities. It is noticed that after the treatment when he dreams again, he feels, clean, whole and hopeful.

Burgess, the linguist and novelist, spins a futuristic tale of violence and reformation. He makes it as one of the most complex novels of the era. Readers become partially, philosophers, theologists and psychologists. As the years go by, the message becomes more relevant, with each new year. There is a bright as well as a dark vision in this dystopian novel. Denna Madden , in her article "Women In Dystopia: Misogyny in *Brave New World, 1984, and A Clockwork Orange*", in *Misogyny in Literature*:

> The future of society of *A Clockwork Orange* is world violent in which the weak are the mercy of the strong. Like *Brave New World* and *1984,* A Clockwork Orange portrays a patriarchal culture in which women are subordinated and peripheral. Women are perceived through the male gaze, in this case that of Fifteen year old delinquent, Alex. While Alex's views may reflect his immaturity. (289)

The world of *A Clockwork Orange* is a, decorative mirror World of London in the early 1960's and also of Russia. Burgess has actually travelled to Russia shortly before writing *A Clockwork Orange* and has noted the phenomenon of the youth gang there. The aim of a dystopian novel is to warn the contemporary society against the possible threats in the future. The dystopian novelists are sure that the patterns of the present day will lead to dystopia in future. Alex gets an opportunity to regain his lost identity. He can decide on his future. It represents both the right of choice and hope for the protagonist.

Burgess' novel paints the future England, that is characterised by violence and state control. Inspite of everything, there is still hope in his description. Just like Orwell and other dystopian novelists, Burgess defines love as the only chance for man to evade his apparently certain fate.

P.D. James known for her detective stories has been hailed as the Queen of crime. She has taken an unexpected turn from her unusual mystery genre to a novel of futuristic dystopia. Her *The Children of Men* has surprised and enthralled her fans. It is written with the same rich blend of keen characterisation, narrative drive and suspense as her great detective stories. Her twelfth book, the dystopian novel has new themes such as loyalty and duty, the corruption of power and redemption through love. It is ingenious, original and irresistible. This readable novel once again confirms her stand as a major novelist. *The Children of Men* stands out from other dystopian science fiction. It is a dark vision of contemporary society. In this novel, the traditional figures of the state authority right from the border patrol guards to the Embassy officials are not to be trusted.

Infertility is the new concept to science fiction writers. Margaret Atwood's has used this science fiction concept in her novel *The Handmaid Tale* P.D. James portrays a world of imminent genetic erasure. No baby is born for eighteen years. They are deeply saddened by the recent death of the youngest person on earth. R. Barash and David Barash in *Dystopian Science Fiction* share a theme of 'Denial of Biology', a denial of human's basic needs. To quote them, "the prospect of genetic continuity is completely absent- a prospect that, 'is the motivation underlying sex, love and indeed everything in the organic world" (1). This novel is set within the entire year of 2021 in and around Oxford. The novel presents a dystopian Britain. Men have lost their fertility for over twenty five years. The novel, part epistolary opens with the protagonist, TheodareFaron, and historian, writing in his diary about the death of the world's youngest person. It seems to be meaningless and sets him in a mood of depression. It is not only Theo but almost the whole world has sunk into depression. XanLypiatt, the self appointed Warden of Britain happens to be the cousin of Theo.

The role of Warden of England represents the ultimate of power in the novel. Xan does not relish the position. But he is unable to retire. He thinks that no one is capable of the role. P.D. James has two themes. One is the baneful effect of tyranny. For example, the unwilling people who do not go to Quietus are forced to go. The second is the human redemption through religious faith. The first part of the novel opens in a subtle manner but finally like an argued case. The year is 2021, the infirm are encouraged to commit suicide. Immigrants are subjected to slavery. For unknown reasons, the worldwide sperm count has reached zero. It is a harrowing race and especially for England to survive and find a solution:

> Theo asked himself how many of the other reforms he might have achieved had he stayed as Xan's adviser. But he knew the answer. He had been powerless then and the Five Fishes were powerless now. If there had been no Omega, these were aims which a man might be prepared to fight for, even to suffer for. But if there had been no Omega, the evils would not exist. (112)

Theo's passivity is shattered when the Five Fishes, a group of revolutionaries approach him for guidance and help. The fact that Theo and Xan happen to be cousins, has given the rebels some sort of hope. Julian one of the Five Fishes, married to Rolf attracts Theo, a lonely man. Theo is confused and has failed in his attempt to convince his cousin Xan the Warden of England. Xan refuses to concede to the demands of Five Fishes. He decides to travel around Europe. On his return, he joins the rebels and helps Julian to deliver her baby, a miracle baby. The circumstances lead to a faceoff between Theo and Xan, "face transfigured with joy and triumph; couldn't have heard his great shout of affirmation, like the shout on the bridge at Woolcombe. But it was with that remembered shout in his ears that he shot Xan through the heart"(238). He hits Xan in the heart. He becomes the new Warden of England, the protector of the baby, thus finding both love and power. *The Children of Men* is certainly arresting with no birth, no babies for a quarter of century starting from 1996.

Theo is not a ready believer. He fears that the world is held together not by love but torment, "by pain, the scream in the throat and the scream in the heart". (225) Theo remains full of doubt even as he stumbles towards belief. The source of James title is found in Miles Coverdale's rendering of 90th psalm, "Thou truest man to destruction again, thou says, come again, ye children of men." Theo's love for Julian is unsentimental. He is even willing to die in order that Julian should live. He becomes a true Christian in death, before confessing his faith in word. P.D. James' novel is most convincing with its hints and gestures at its deep truths. This novel remains the most provocative novel. The novel ends not moralistically but miraculously through an act at once human and holy.

Huxley's *Brave New World* shows that the concept of Utopia is gradually detiorating. He declares that the problem is that knowledge has destroyed the value of life. *Brave New World* describes a sexual regime which resembles what one rules today. The starting point is the life in the hatchery where the abundance of technology and knowledge prevails. Test tube babies are produced in thousands without any parents to provide guidance and show love. There is space only for sleeping, teaching and conditioning. They are brain washed to learn everything they need to know to live their lives. Theodore Dalrymple, in his article "The Dystopian Imagination", points out that,

> In Huxley's dystopia as among liberals today, enlightment and permissiveness are synonymous. The Director of Hatcheries and Conditioning tells his students it was in the old, unenlightened times:
>
> > …what I'm going to tell you ; he said, 'may sound incredible. But then, when you're not accustomed to history, most facts about the past do sound incredible'. (29)

Men are taught to think that women are pieces of meat and sex is completely recreational. The writers have attempted to persuade the readers in subset of dystopian novels: the drug dystopia. Huxley in the most successful *Brave New World* makes it a point in which drugs, fictional and real, figure prominently. John Hickman in his article,

”Rise and Fall of the Twentieth Century Drug Dystopia” says that, “Huxley condemns recreational drug use with the same intensity as he does anti- intellectualism, mindless popular entertainments, sexual promiscuity, materialism, and eugenically enforced race and class inequality” (5). Huxley’s novel is either a perfect world utopia or it is a nasty dystopia. He has created a dystopian society and that society does not give any credits to past history. It is formed on fear and revulsions. This secular culture has characteristics such as economics, technology, and its dedicated to the pursuit of sexual appetites. He invents the perfect narcotics, soma and the feelies for the dystopian year of Ford.

Orwell’s *Nineteen Eighty-Four* is generally remarked as a criticism of the Stalinism in the Soviet Union or as a criticism of Communist hysteria in the West or even both. Orwell deconstructs three super power states. Orwell’s book offers a prophetic view of modern politics. Once again, recalling the words of Theodre,

> Winston Smith copies a passage from a child’s history textbook: In the old days, before the glorious Revolution, London was a dark, dirty, miserable place where hardly anybody had enough to eat and where hundreds and thousands of poor people had no boots on their feet and not even a roof to sleep under... (29)

Orwell’s *Nineteen Eighty-Four* is a dystopian novel. It portrays a society ruled by a dictator. The Oceanian province of Air Strip One is a world of perceptual war. It is ruled by the political Party, simply called The Party. The citizens are subordinates to the state. So the Party manipulates and controls humanity. The protagonist Winston Smith works in the Ministry of Truth. This civil servant functions as the party propaganda man. He has revised historical records to render the Party as omnipresent and as always correct. He is disillusionsed and goes to the point of seeking rebellion against Big Brother. Orwell is a socialist, a keen critic of imperialism, fascism, Stalinism and capitalism. He has picturiesd the socio-political conditions of his time and also the problem of human freedom. His plain and simple style is very effective. He has received far and wide reputation and recognition. His political shrewdness and sharp satires have placed him along with the best writers. Orwell's *Nineteen Eighty Four* is regarded as a literary political fiction. Many of its terms and concepts, such as "double think", "thoughtcrime", "newspeak", and 'memory hole' have become contemporary vernacular.

Anthony Burgess' *A Clockwork Orange* is considered to be a brilliant novel and a savage satire. It is a frightening fable about good and evil meaning of human freedom. Burgess states in the 'introduction' of the novel:

> …by definition, a human being is endowed with free will. He can use this tochoose between good and evil. If he can only perform good or only performevil, then he is a clockwork orange—meaning that he has the appearance ofan organism lovely with colour and juice, but is in fact only a clockwork toywound up by God or the Devil or (since this is increasingly replacing both)the Almighty State. (ix)

The central character, Alex a fifteen year old droog of this 1963 classic, is vicious. It is Anthony Burgess' nightmarish visions of the future. The criminals take over the dark. Alex talks in a brutal invented slang that brilliantly renders his and his friends a social pathology. Burgess describes this novel as a socially pre-dystopian novel in the beginning of the totalitarianism. He exposes the raw agenda of dystopia, of social controls, and efficiency over the human nature. Burgess shares many characteristics to those of dystopian novels like *Nineteen Eighty –Four* and *Brave New World.* Heller and Kiraly, in their article, "Behavior Modification: A Classroom Clockwork Orange?", state that, "… A Clockwork Orange portrays a detached, uncaring society where ultra violence is the only method of saying, 'I am alive"(199).

P.D. James' *The Children of Men* picturises a world with no children and no future. Her vividness of characterisation and mastery of storytelling helps the smooth flow of the story till the end. The plot of the dystopian novel is about a man's journey to love and meaning in life. This dystopian novel is said to be about mass infertility. Her novels explore a dystopia that is not dominated by the totalitarian regime. With the advancement of science and technology, the writers can foretell the formation of dystopian societies all over the world. It is their moral duty to warn the impending and unavoidable destruction and disillusionment. The use of drugs, dictatorship, violence and infertility are the major concern of them. The scope for dystopian fiction has flourished and many British novelists have excelled in making use of this genre.

All the dystopian novels are unique not because of the novelists or their writing style. They warn against the perils of the machine society in general. In the nineteen fifties, the British and American novelists warn a peril of the then contemporary enemy.

Huxley and Orwell have depicted through their writings that any form of manipulation of human mind, human emotions will definitely lead to a dystopian future. The new dystopian culture is the government's efforts to take control over the thoughts and lives of the people. The dystopian genre is a traditionally bleak and depressing one. The danger and domination of the totalitarian regimes are a timely and effective warning, especially for the future generation. Individuality and freedom are at stake.

Huxley's *Brave New World*, Orwell's *Nineteen Eighty -Four*, Burgess' *A Clockwork Orange* and P.D.James' *The Children of Men* are accepted as the masterpieces of English dystopian literature. All these dystopian novels portray the novelists' concerns about the future world. They belong to a different period of the twentieth century, with different background and experience. But they have shared the same urge to warn people, the threat to their freedom, brainwashing and the influence of techniques to control them. The depiction, approach and solution offered by the novelists differ. Huxley's society based on genetic engineering picturises happy individuals worshipping consumerism. The society imagined by Orwell has to live with fear, repression and permanent control. Anthony Burgess is totally against the techniques of brainwashing. More importance is to be given to free will and capacity for moral choice. Different individuals react differently to brainwashing.

Some people succumb to devoted enthusiasm. Many people opt for solitary life and some people go for rebellion and revolt. Brainwashing proves to be fatal for many. It disintegrates the personality. Brainwashing and influence techniques lead to totalitarianism. Even in liberal societies it is used as a powerful tool to shape and to manufacture beliefs. Huxley's John, Orwell's Smith, and Burgess' Alex and the individuals living in twenty first century should be alert. Their free will should not be threatened of brainwashing. This kind of future may be utopian unrealistic. Ignoring and not protesting will produce dystopian societies. Their apathy and intolerance bring oppression. The message of these novels is that one should not be indifferent to future. This type of science fiction has real and profound meanings. These satirical novels should be taken as severe warning. They are not only warnings but didactic messages. The government and authorities should not be allowed to have the upper hand. This is power of thinking, power of dystopian novels and the power and reach of literature. Literature has tremendous and unlimited power and influence over nations and citizens. As people are forced to live in a dystopian world, these novels help to escape from 'ignorance and being controlled'.

Thus the discussed novels signal not only a frightening future but also gives a warning for the individual to be alert. The readers should take these dystopian novels which ring an alarming bell of the society, in the days to come in a serious sense and prepare themselves to meet the challenging future. Man, being a social animal ought to be more concerned about the society he lives in. Every problem, when analysed well can be solved in a fruitful manner. Once upon a time, man has been dying to discover and invent scientifically and walk with pomp and pride on the path of technological advancement. The same science seems to strangle the neck of humankind, of late. Man may get choked completely in the future and that's what these dystopian novels are trying to foretell with a deep insight of analysis. Hence, the preventive measures have to be taken in the most serious and emphatic manner. The last novel *The Children of Men* suggests a ray of hope towards its end. In general, the dystopian novels give a frightening picture of the future and so the steps to be taken to overcome the fearful atmosphere of the future societies, can be taken up for further study and research. More novels should be written on this basis and those type of books should be brought to the notice of the readers so as to enhance their social awakening.

Works Consulted

Primary source:

Burgess, Anthony. *A Clockwork Orange*. U.K: W.W Norton& Company, 1962. Print.

Huxley, Aldous. *Brave New World.* U.K: Vintage, 1932.Print.

James,P.D. *The Children of Men*. U.K: Vintage, 1992. Print.

Orwell, George. *Nineteen Eighty-Four*. U.K: Modern Penguin. 1947. Print.

Secondary source:

Arendt, Hannah. "The Origins of Totalitarianism." *On Viloence*. Ed. Bruce. B. Lawrence and Aisha. U.S: Duke University Press, 2007. Print.

Atkins, John. *Aldous Huxley: A Literary Study*. London: John Cadler, 1956. Print.

Baccolini, Raffaella. "Gender and Genre in the Feminist Critical Dystopias of Katherine Burdekin, Margaret Atwood, and Octavia Butler." *Future Females, the Next Generation.* Ed.Marleen S. Barr. Lanham: Rowman and Littlefield, 2000. Print.

Booker, Keith M. *Dystopian Literature: A Theory and Research Guide*. U.K: Greenwood Presst, 1994. Print.

Booker, M. Keith. "African Literature and the World System: Dystopian Fiction, Collective Experience, and the Postcolonial Condition." *Research in African Literatures.* 26, no 4 winter 1995. Print.

Brander, Lawrence. *Aldous Huxley: A Critical Study*. London: Athlone Press,1968. Print.

Burgess, Anthony. "Clockwork Marmalade." *The Listener*, Vol.87, No.2238, London: February 17, 1972.

Claeys, Gregory. *Utopian Literature.* Cambridge: Cambridge UP, 2010. Print.

Claeys, Gregory. "The Origin of Dystopian: Wells, Huxley and Orwell". *The Cambridge Companion to Utopian literature.* Cambridge: Cambridge UP. 2010. Print.

Colmer, John. "Utopian Fantasy." *Coleridge to Catch-22: Images of Society.* London: Macmillan Press. 1978. Print.

Corea, Gena. *The Mother Machine*. London: The Women's Press, 1988. Print.

Cullinan, John. "Anthony Burgess A Clockwork Orange: Two Versions." *English Language Notes*. Vol. IX, No. 4, June, 1972.

DeVitis, A.A. "England, Education, and the Future." *Anthony Burgess*. New York: Twayne, 1972. Print.

Dalrymple, Theodare. "The Dystopian Imagination." *Dark Horizons.* London: Routledge Publishers, 2002. Print.

Davison, Peter. *George Orwell, Nineteen Eighty- Four: The Facsimile of the Extant Manuscript.* Weston, MA: M&S Press, 1984. Print.

Dawson, Cheney Margaret. "Huxley Turns Propagandist." *New York Herald Tribune*. New York: February 7, 1932. Print.

Deutscher, Isaac. "1984- The Mysticism of Cruelty." *Russia in Transition and Other Essays.* London: Hamish Hamilton. 1955. Print.

Evans O. Robert. "Nadast: The Argot and Its Implications I Anthony Burgess A Clockwork Orange." *Journal of Modern Literature*. Vol. No.3. New York: March, 1971.

Firchow, Peter Edgerly. "A Study of Aldous Huxley's Brave New World." *The End of Utopia.* London: Bucknell University Press, 1984. Print.

Firchow, Peter. *Aldous Huxley: Satirist and Novelist.* USA: University of Minnesota Press, 1972. Print.

Fortunati, Vita, and Raymond Trousson. *Dictionary of Literary Utopias.* Paris: Honore Champion, 2000. Print.

Fredic, Warburg. "Publisher's Report." *George Orwell: The Critical Heritage.* London : Routledge and Kegan Paul, 1975. Print.

Frye, Northrop. *Anatomy of Criticism: Four Essays*. Princeton: Princeton University Press, 1957. Print.

Fukuyama, Francis. *The End of History and Last Man*. New York: Free Press, 1992. Print.

Gottlieb, Erika. *Dystopian Fiction East and West: Universe of Terror and Trial*. Canada: McGill-Queen's Press, 2001. Print.

Greenblat, Stephen. "Aldous Huxley." *Three Modern Satirists: Waugh, Orwell, and Huxley.* London: Yale University Press, 1965. Print.

Hazlitt, Hendry. "What's Wrong with Utopia?" *The Nation.* New York, No, 3476, February 17, 1932. Print.

Hickman, John. "When science fiction writers used fictional drugs: rise and fall of the twentieth-century drug dystopia." *Utopian Studies.* 20.1 (2009): 141+. Literature Resource Center. Web. 18 Mar 2013. Print.

Huntington, John. "Utopian and Anti Utopian Logic: H.G Wells and His Successors." *Science Fiction Studies* 9. No.2 USA: July 1982. Print.

Huxley, Aldous, and Donald Watt. *The Critical Heritage*. London: Routledge & K. Paul, 1975. Print.

Hyman, Edgar Stanley. "Anthony Burgess Clockwork." *The New Leader*. Vol. XLVI. USA: January 7, 1963. Print.

Jameson, Fredric. *Archaeologies of the Future: The Desire Called Utopia and Other Science Fictions*, London: Verso, 2005. Print.

Karim's . *On Violence*: *A Reader*. USA: Duke University Press, 1951. Print.

Koestler, Arthur. *Darkness at Noon*. New York: Bantam, 1966. Print.

Kumar, Krishan. *Utopia and Anti-Utopia in Modern Times.* Oxford: Blackwell, 1987. Print.

… *The Dystopian Impulse in Modern Literature: Fiction as Social Criticism*. Oxford: Blackwell, 1994. Print.

Larsen, J. Randy & David M. Buss. *Personality Psychology.* New York: McGraw- Hill Companies, 2011 Print.

Lobb, Edward. "The Subversion of Drama in Huxley's 'Brave New World'." *The International Fiction Review*. Vol. 11, No. 2, London: Summer. 1984. Print.

Lucas, W. Scott. "An Analysis of Nineteen Eighty –Four." In *Twentieth- Century Literary Criticism.* Vol. 129, Eds . Scott Darga and Linda Pavlovski. Farmington Hills, Mich: The Gale Group,2003.

Madden Deanna, "Women In Dystopia: Misogyny in Brave New World, 1984, and A Clockwork Orange." *Misogyny in Literature: An Essay Collection*. Ed. Katherine Anne Ackley, New York: Garland Publishing, 1992. Print.

Mitchell Julian, "Horrorshow on Amis Avenue." *The Spectator*. Vol.5, No. 6986, London: May 18, 1962. Print.

Morris K. Robert, "The Bitter Fruits of Freedom." *The Consolation of Ambiguity: An Essay on the Novels of Anthony Burgess*. London: University of Missouri Press, 1971. Print.

Moylan, Tom. *Demand the Impossible: Science Fiction and the Utopian Imagination.* London: Methue, 1986. Print.

… [Thomas Patrick]. *Scraps of the Untainted Sky: Science Fiction, Utopia, Dystopia*. Boulder Colo: Westview Press, 2000. Print.

Passer & Smith. *Psychology. Frontiers and Application.* New York: McGraw-Hill. 2001. Print.

PhiloM.Buck, Jr., "Sight to the Blind: Aldous Huxley." *Directions in Contemporary Literature.* Oxford: Oxford University Press, Inc., 1942. Print.

Pritchard H. William, "The Novels of Anthony Burgess." *The Massachusetts Review.* Vol. 7, No. 7, No.3, London: Summer, 1996.

R.T. Oerton, "The End of the Beginning." *The Twentieth Century*. Vol. 175, First Quarter, 1967. Print.

Rabinnovitz Rubin, "Mechanism vs. Organism: Anthony Burgess' A Clockwork Orange." *Modern Fiction Studies*. Vol. 24, No. 4, London: Winter, 1978-1979. Print.

Robson, W.W. *Modern English Literature.* Oxford: Oxford University Press, 1970.

Roger, Fowler. *The Language of George Orwell.* London: Macmillan, 1995. Print.

Rorty, Richard. "The Last Intellectual In Europe: Orwell on Cruelty." *Contingency, Irony, and Solidarity.* Cambridge: Cambridge University Press, 1989. Print.

Rossenfeld, Issac. 'Decency and Death.' *Partisan Review.* XVII. May 1950. Print.

Russell, Bertrand, 'Symptoms of Orwell's 1984.' *Portraits from Memory.* London and New York: Separate Publications, 1956. Print.

Sargent, Lyman Tower. "The Three Faces of Utopianism Revisited." *Utopian Studies,* Vol.5, nr.1, 1994.

Stein, Karen F. "Margaret Atwood's The Handmaid Tale: Scheheazade in Dystopia." *University of Toronto Quarterly.* 61, no.2 winter 1991-1992. Print.

Steinhoff, William. *George Orwell and the Origin of '1984'.* Ann Arbor: University of Michigan Press, 1975. Print.

Timothy, Ash Garton. "Orwell for Our Time." *The Guardian*. 5 May 2001. Print.

W. Adorno,Teodor. *Aldous Huxley and Utopia*. Cambridge: The MIT Press, 1981. Print.

Watt, Donald. *Aldous Huxley*: *The Critical Heritage.* London: Routledge and Kegan Paul, 1975. Print.

Wood, C Ralph. "Rapidly Rises The Morning Tide: An Essay on P.D. James The Children of Men." *Theology Today*. July 1994; 51, 2; Research Library. Print.

Woodcock, George. "Dawn and the Darkest Hour". *A Study of Aldous Huxley.* London: Faber and Faber, 1975. Print.

<http://biography.yourdictionary.com/anthony-burgess>

<https://www.kirkusreviews.com/book-reviews/pd-james/the-children-of-men/>